Copyright © 2020 by Steven Kinslow

All rights reserved. No part of this publication may be reproduced, distributed, or transmitted in any form or by any means, including photocopying, recording, or other electronic or mechanical methods, without the prior written permission of the publisher.

Mapping Mind Connections

001 Ellipses Cover

Generate and brainstorm surprising new

connections or mind maps, and plan new ideas.

Use this book for simplifying large discussions,

brainstorming, managing teams and projects

Remember, the pages in this journal are just

starting points and guides. Add your own

connections and ideas as you progress.

IDEAS:

PROMPTS:

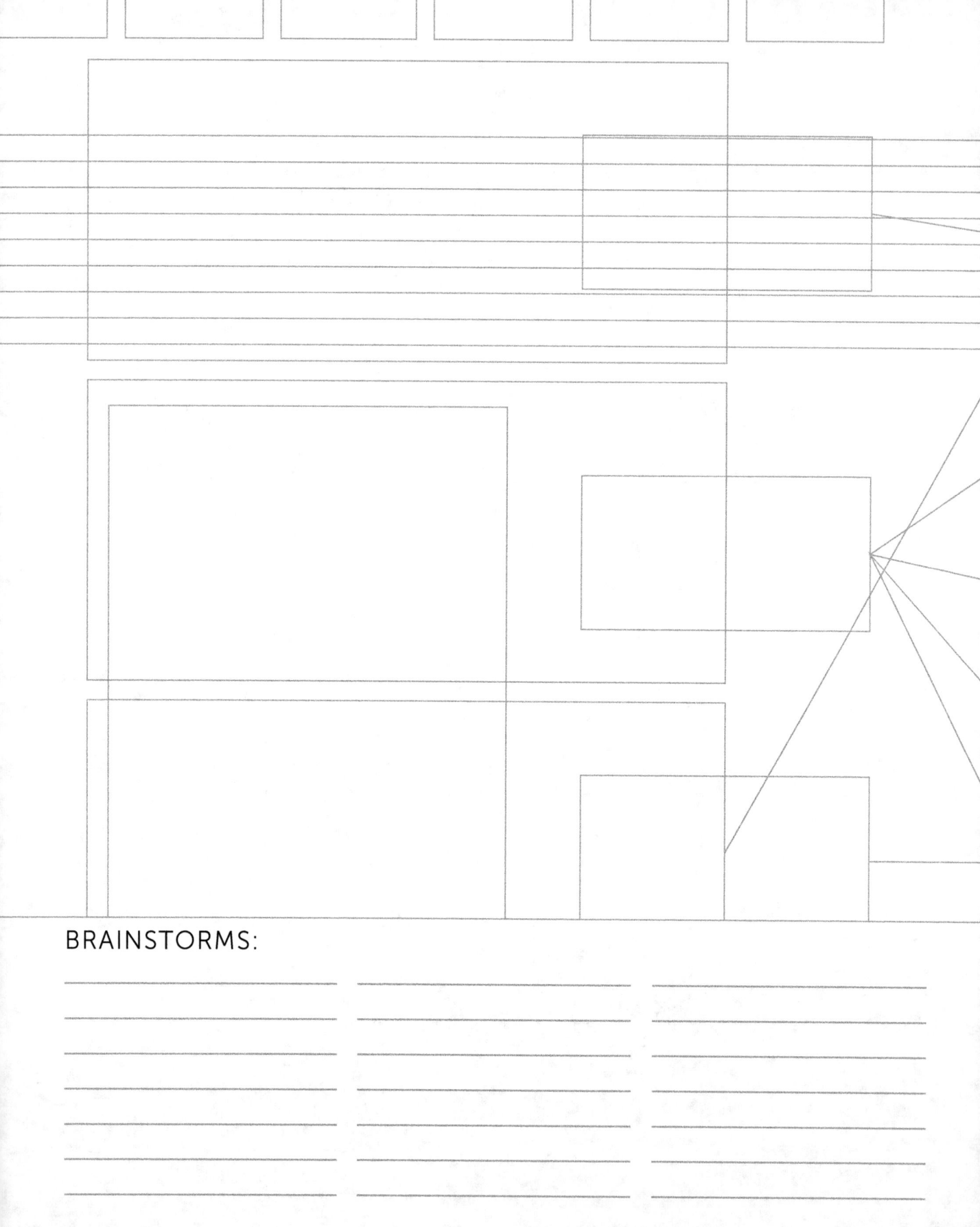

BRAINSTORMS:

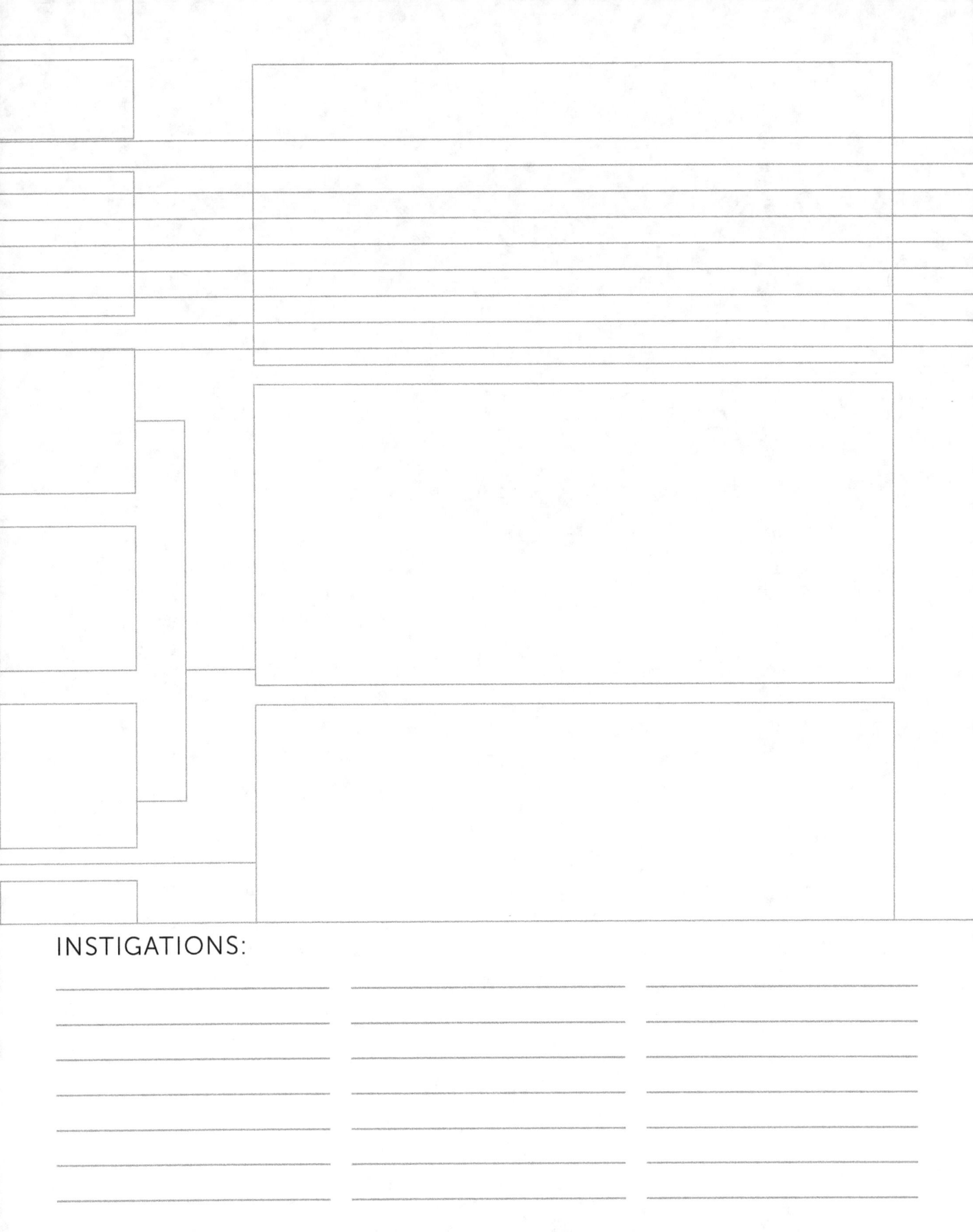

INSTIGATIONS:

LEFT FIELD:

RIGHT FIELD:

IN THE BOX:

OUT OF THE BOX:

IDEAS:

PROMPTS:

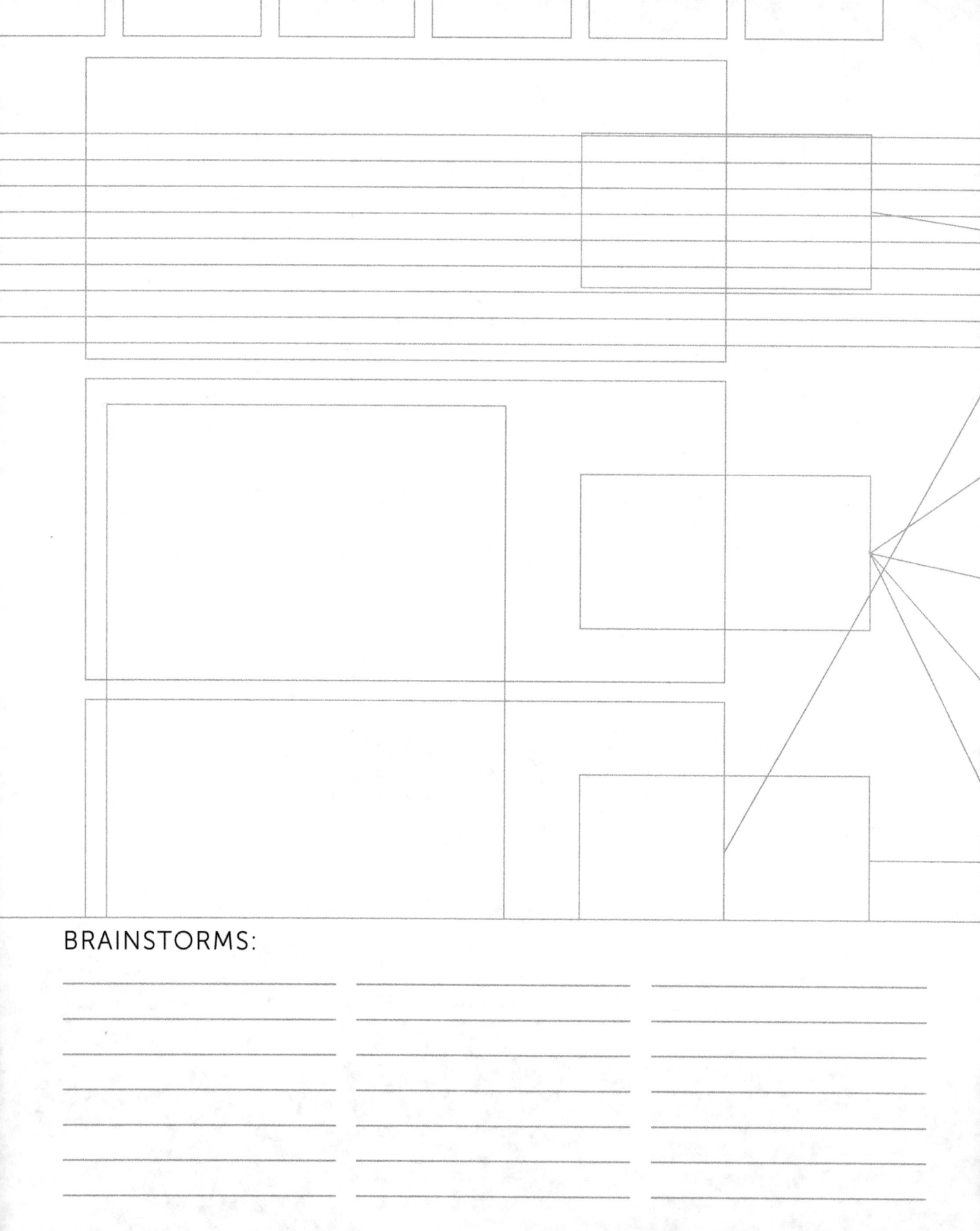

BRAINSTORMS:

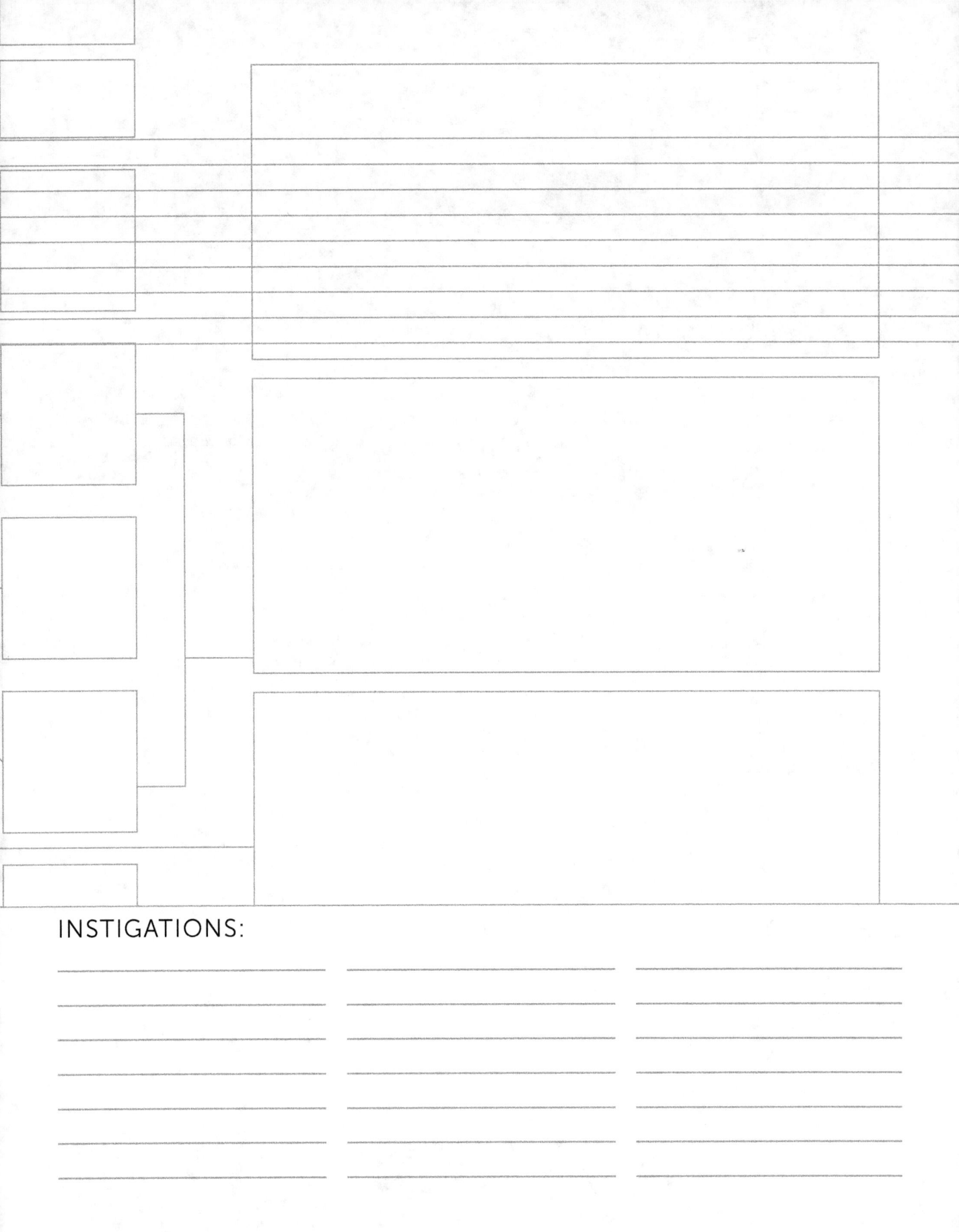

INSTIGATIONS:

LEFT FIELD:

RIGHT FIELD:

IN THE BOX:

OUT OF THE BOX:

IDEAS:

PROMPTS:
_____ _____ _____
_____ _____ _____
_____ _____ _____
_____ _____ _____
_____ _____ _____
_____ _____ _____
_____ _____ _____

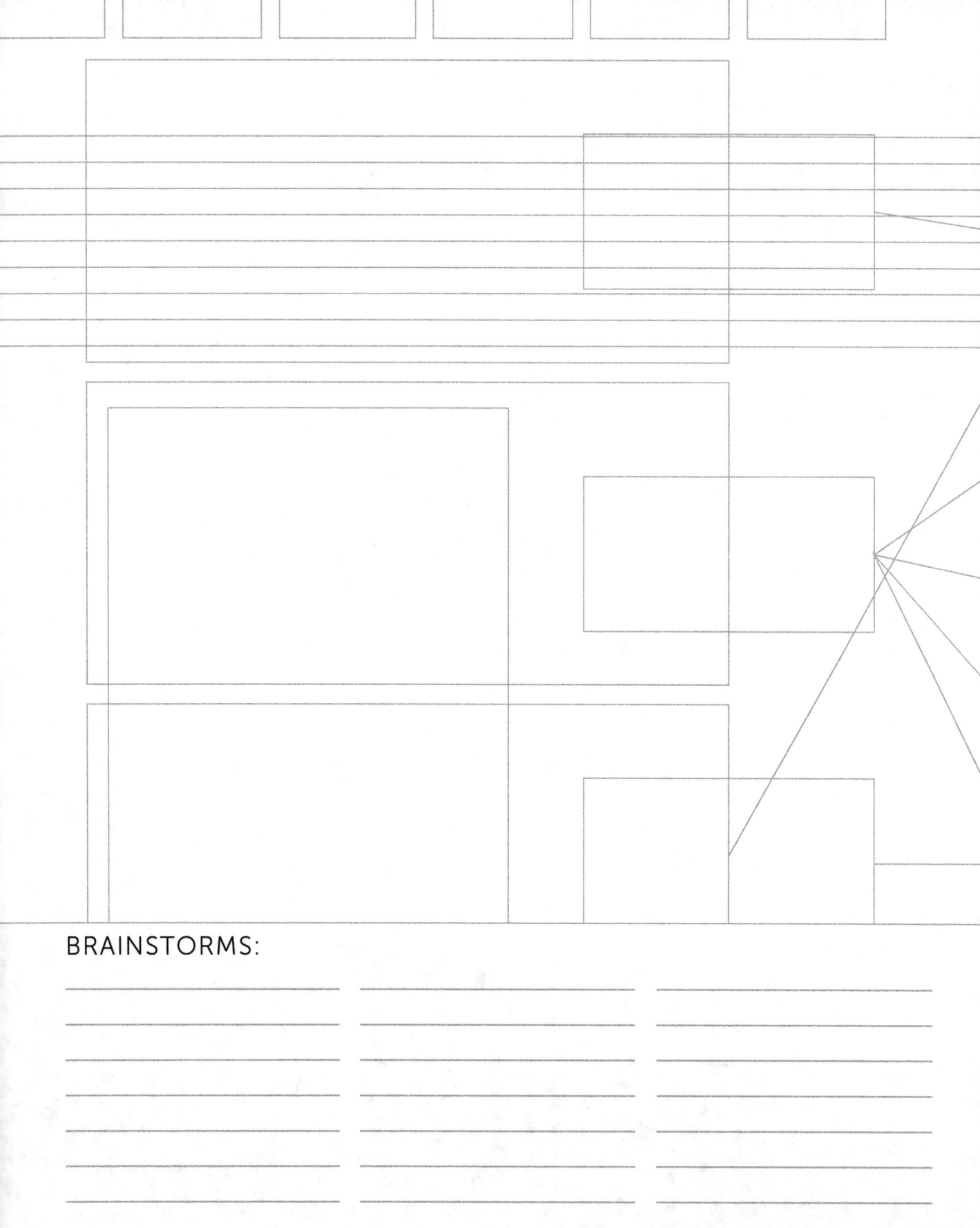

BRAINSTORMS:

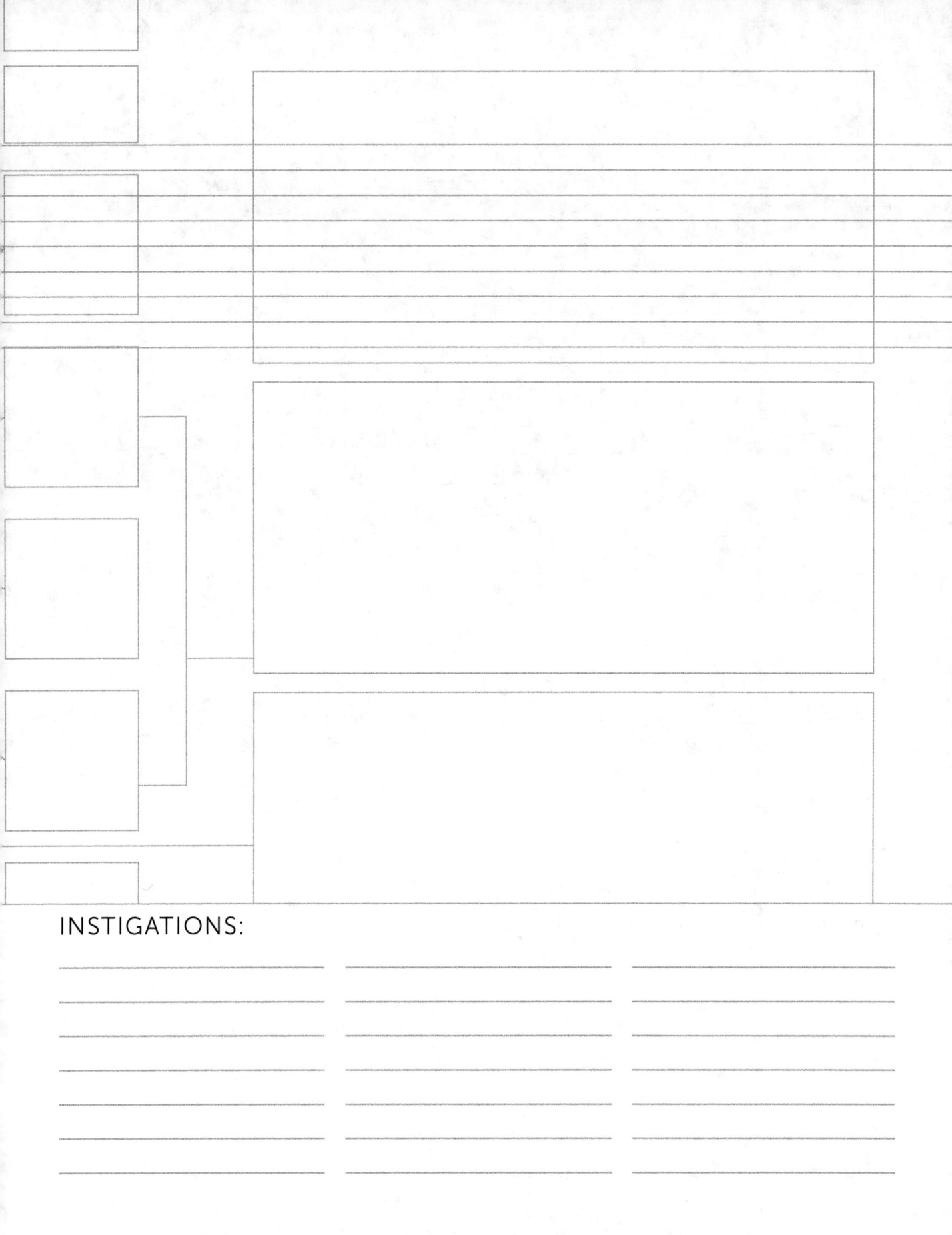

INSTIGATIONS:

LEFT FIELD:

RIGHT FIELD:

IN THE BOX:

OUT OF THE BOX:

IDEAS:

PROMPTS:

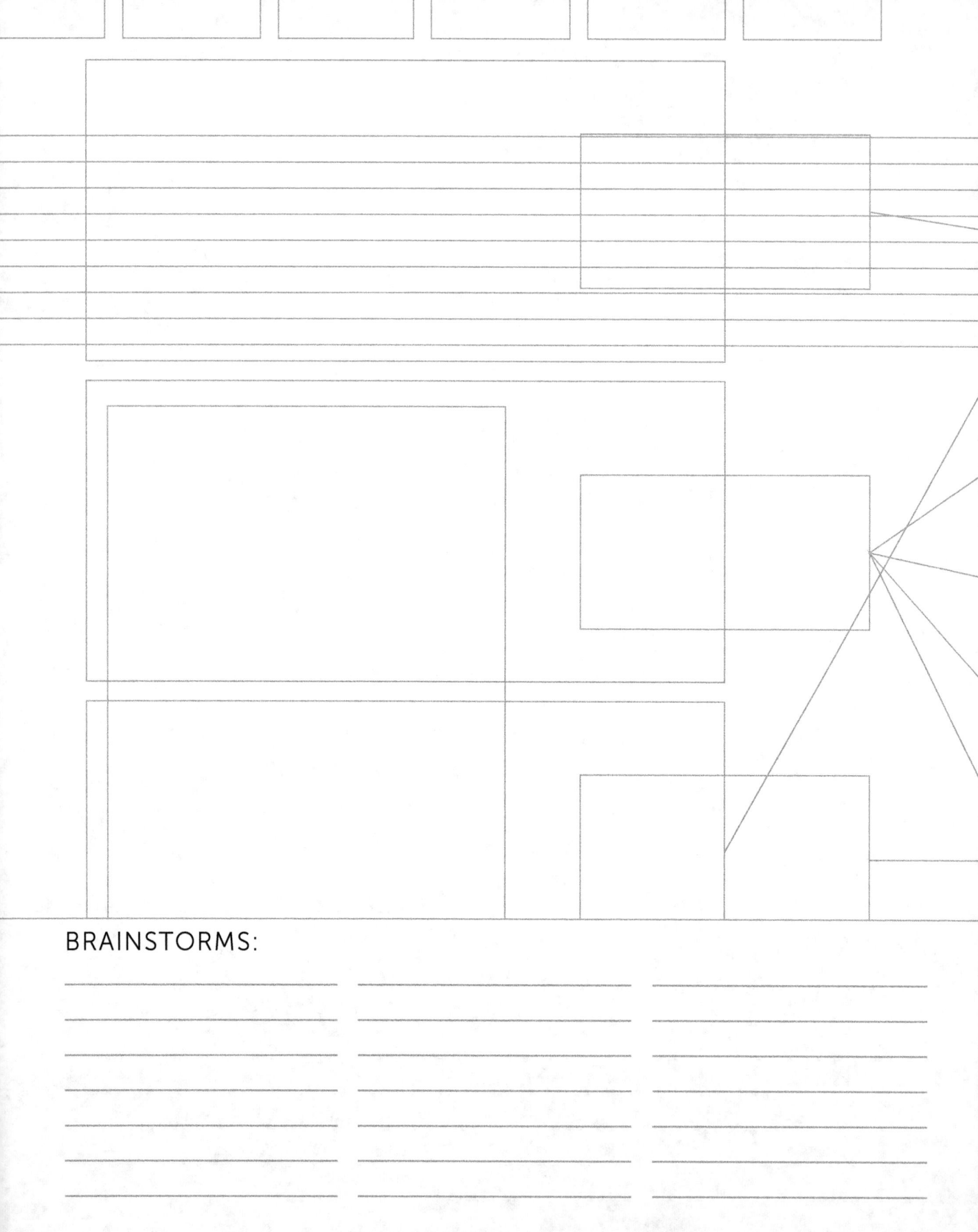

BRAINSTORMS:

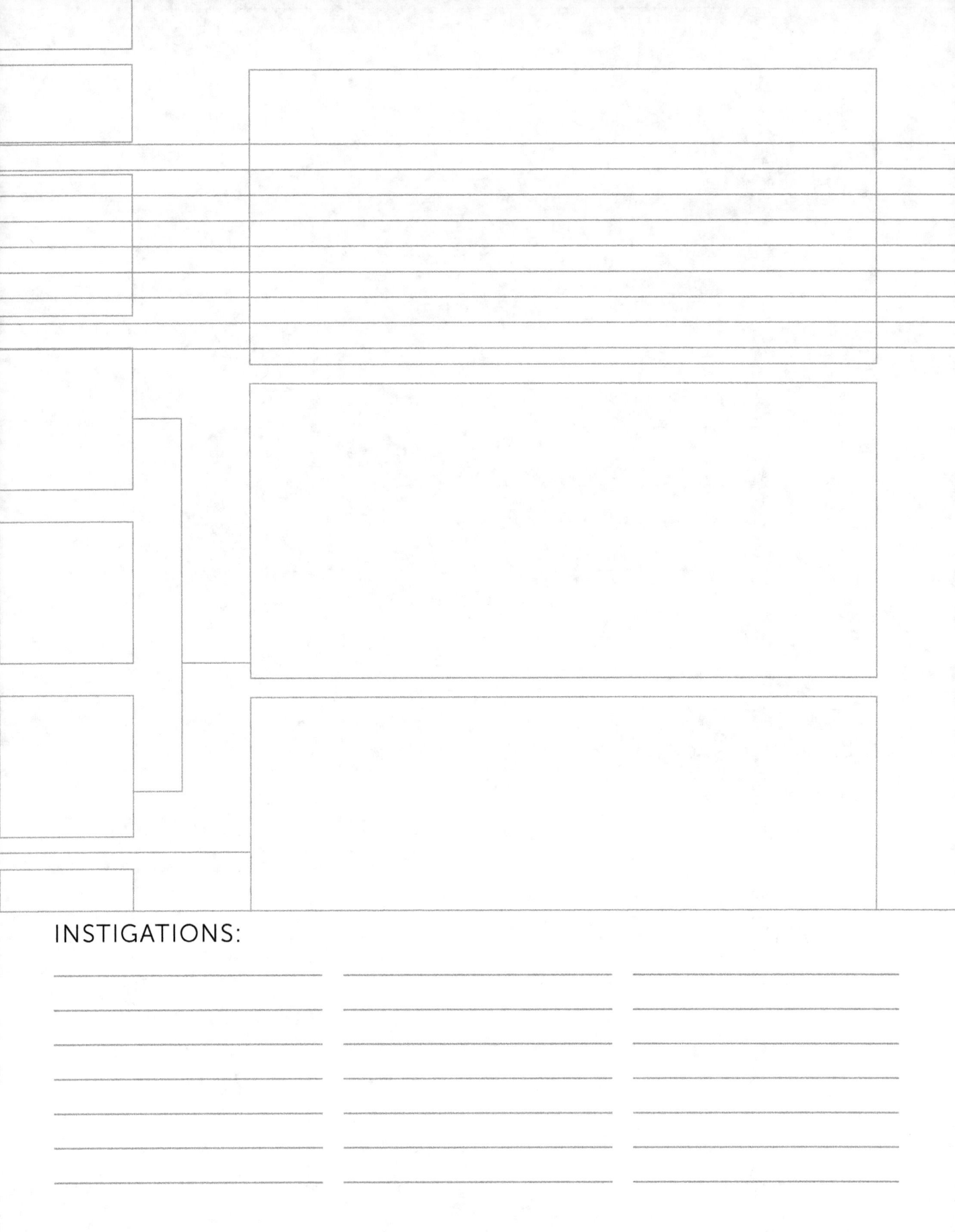

INSTIGATIONS:

LEFT FIELD:

RIGHT FIELD:

IN THE BOX:

OUT OF THE BOX:

IDEAS:

PROMPTS:

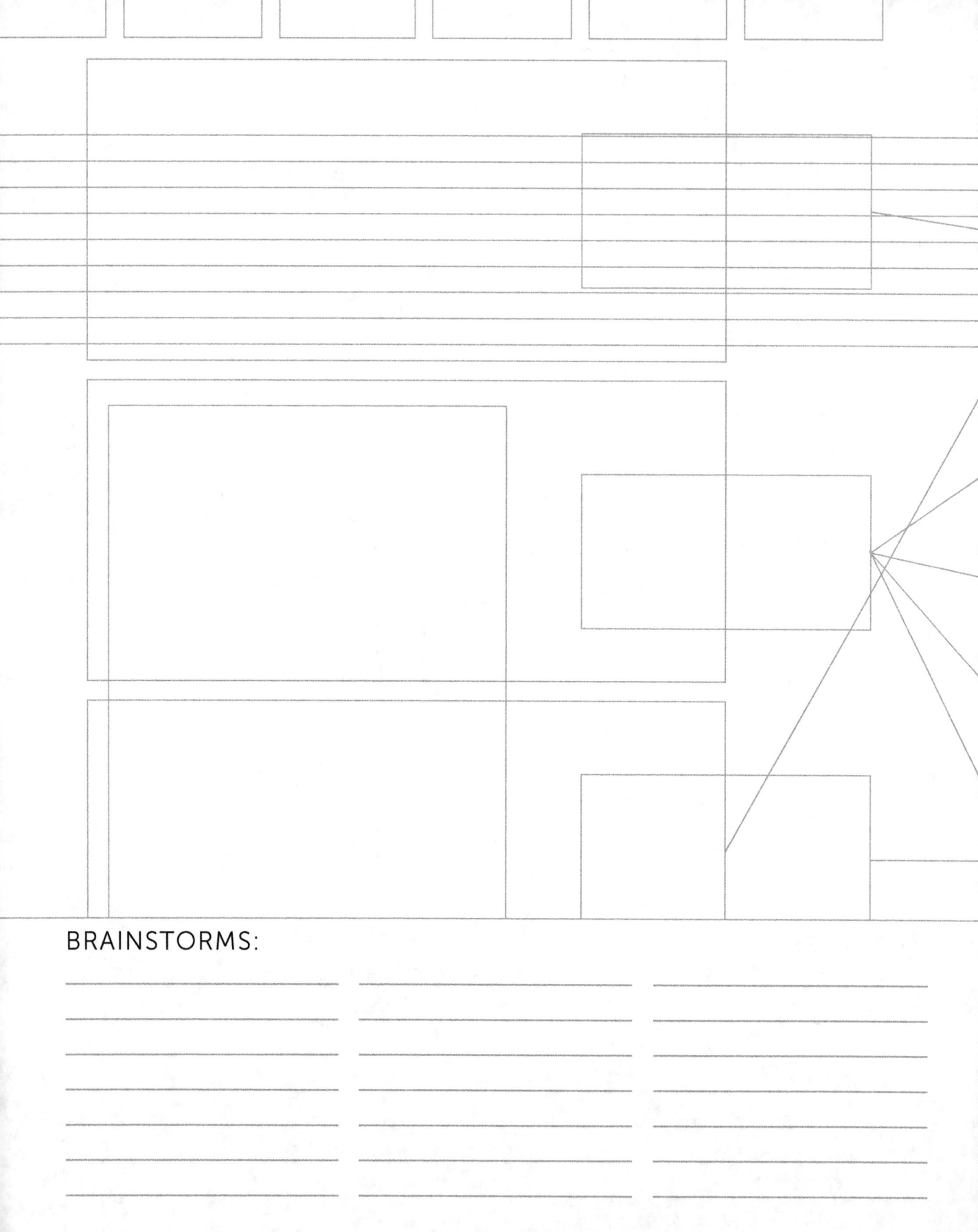

BRAINSTORMS:

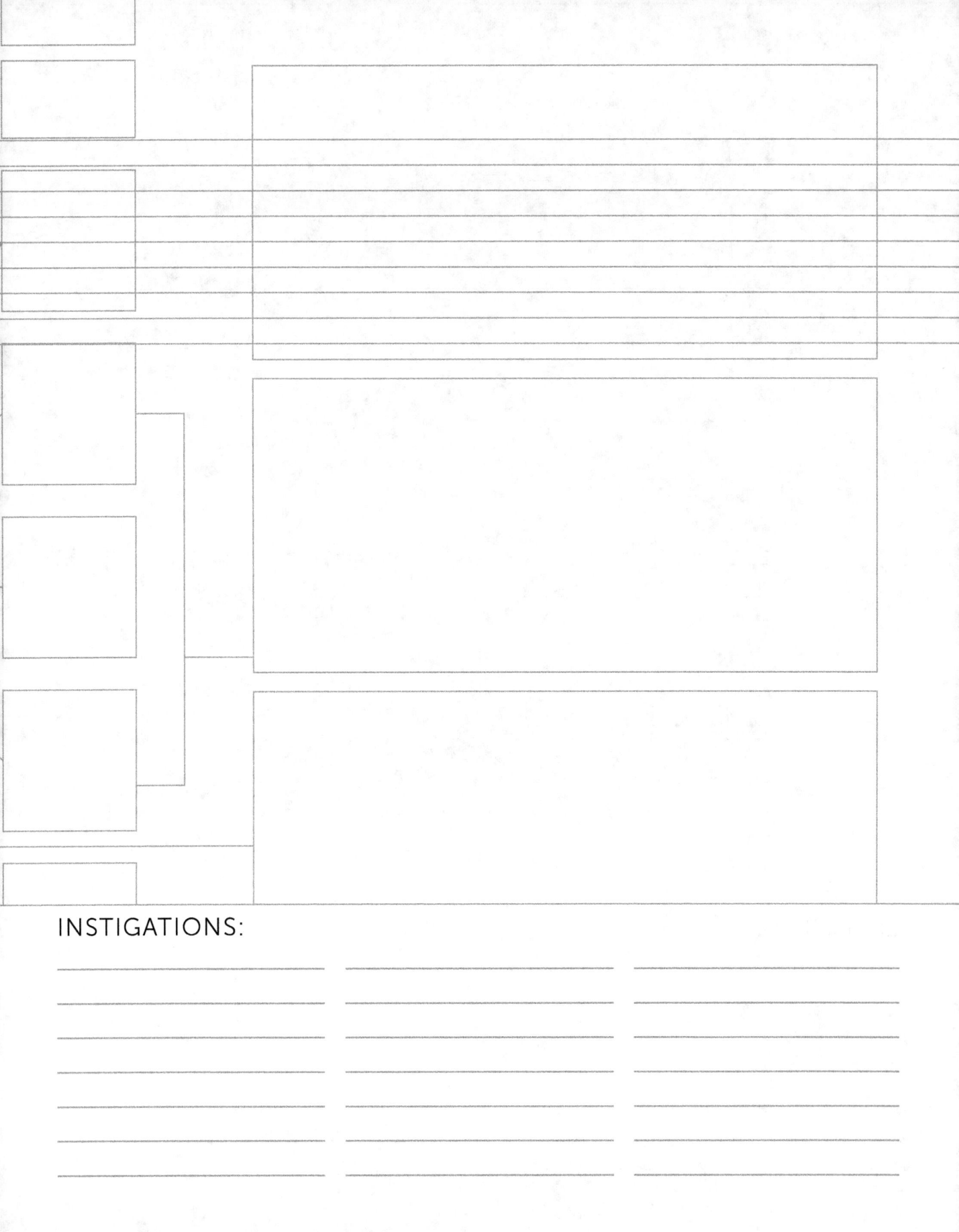

INSTIGATIONS:

LEFT FIELD:

RIGHT FIELD:

IN THE BOX:

OUT OF THE BOX:

LEFT FIELD:

RIGHT FIELD:

IDEAS:

PROMPTS:

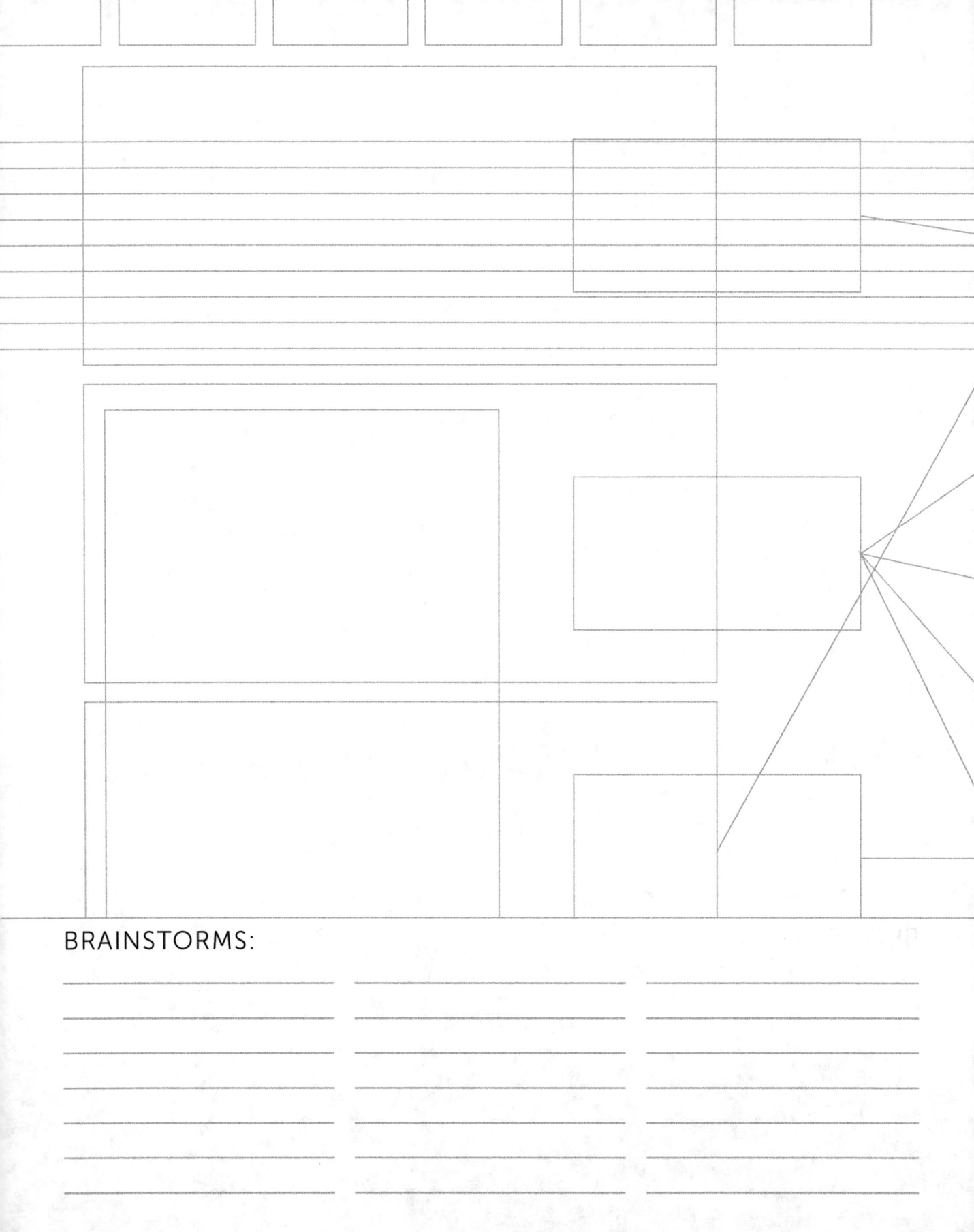

BRAINSTORMS:

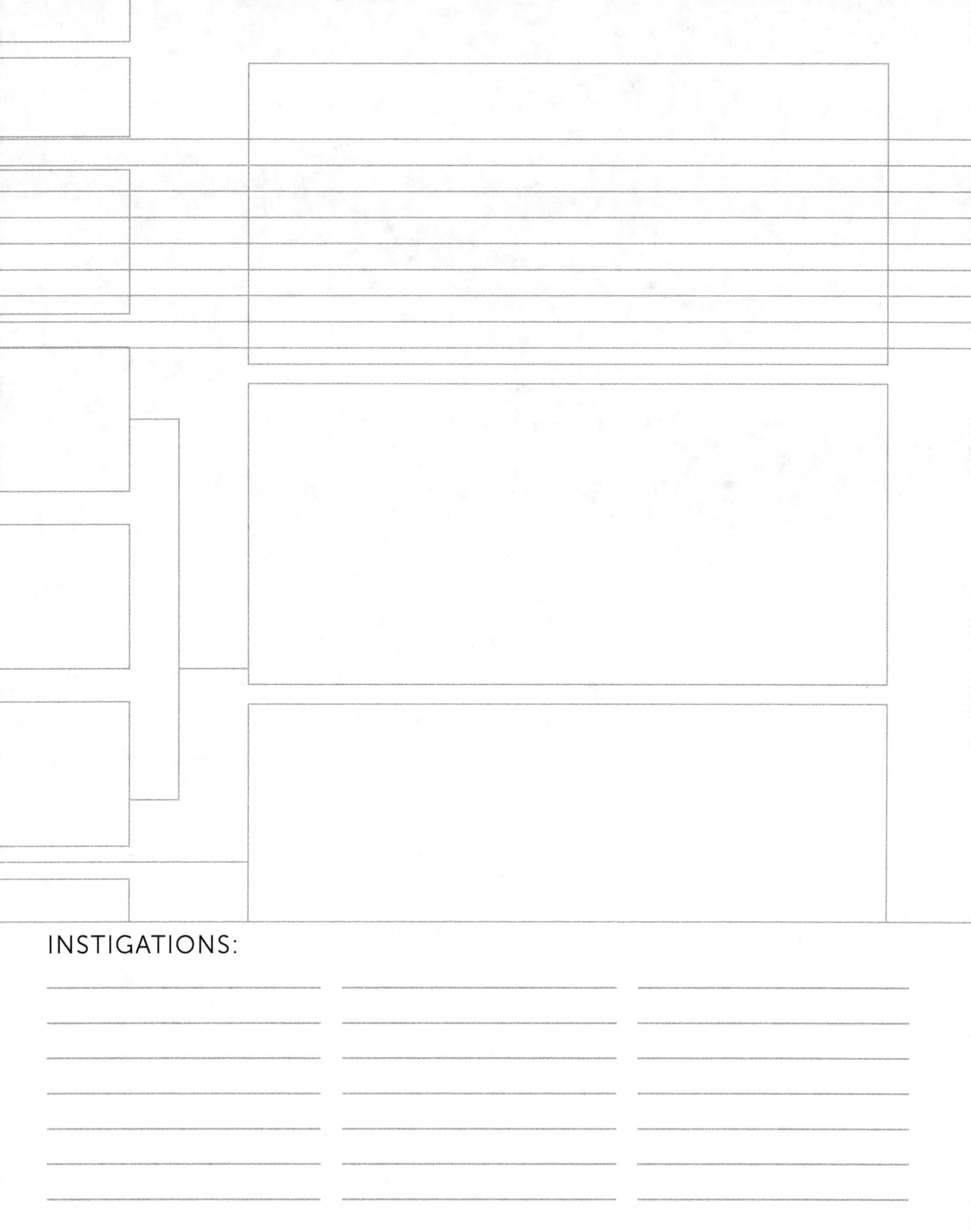

INSTIGATIONS:

LEFT FIELD:

RIGHT FIELD:

IN THE BOX:

OUT OF THE BOX:

IDEAS:

PROMPTS:

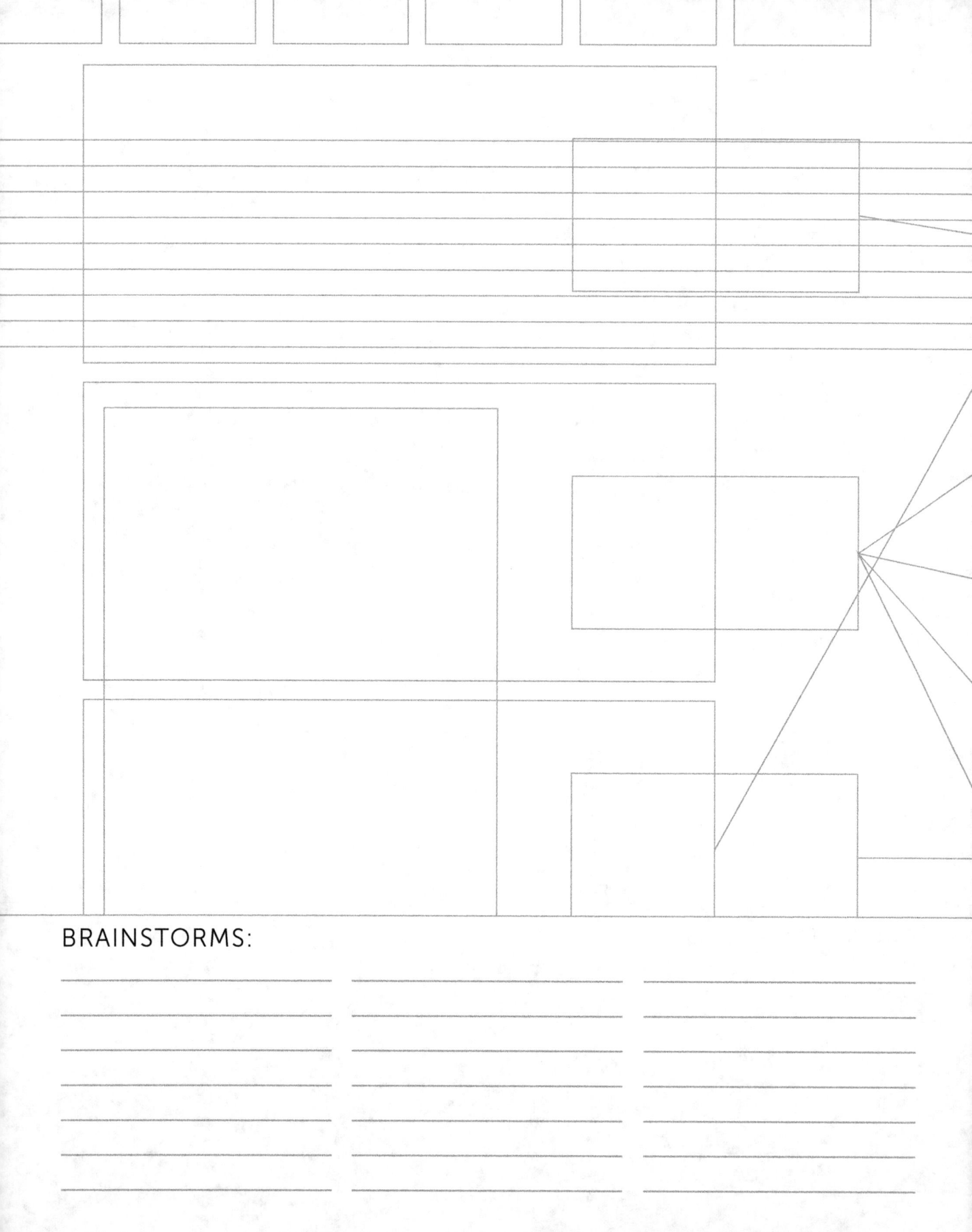

BRAINSTORMS:

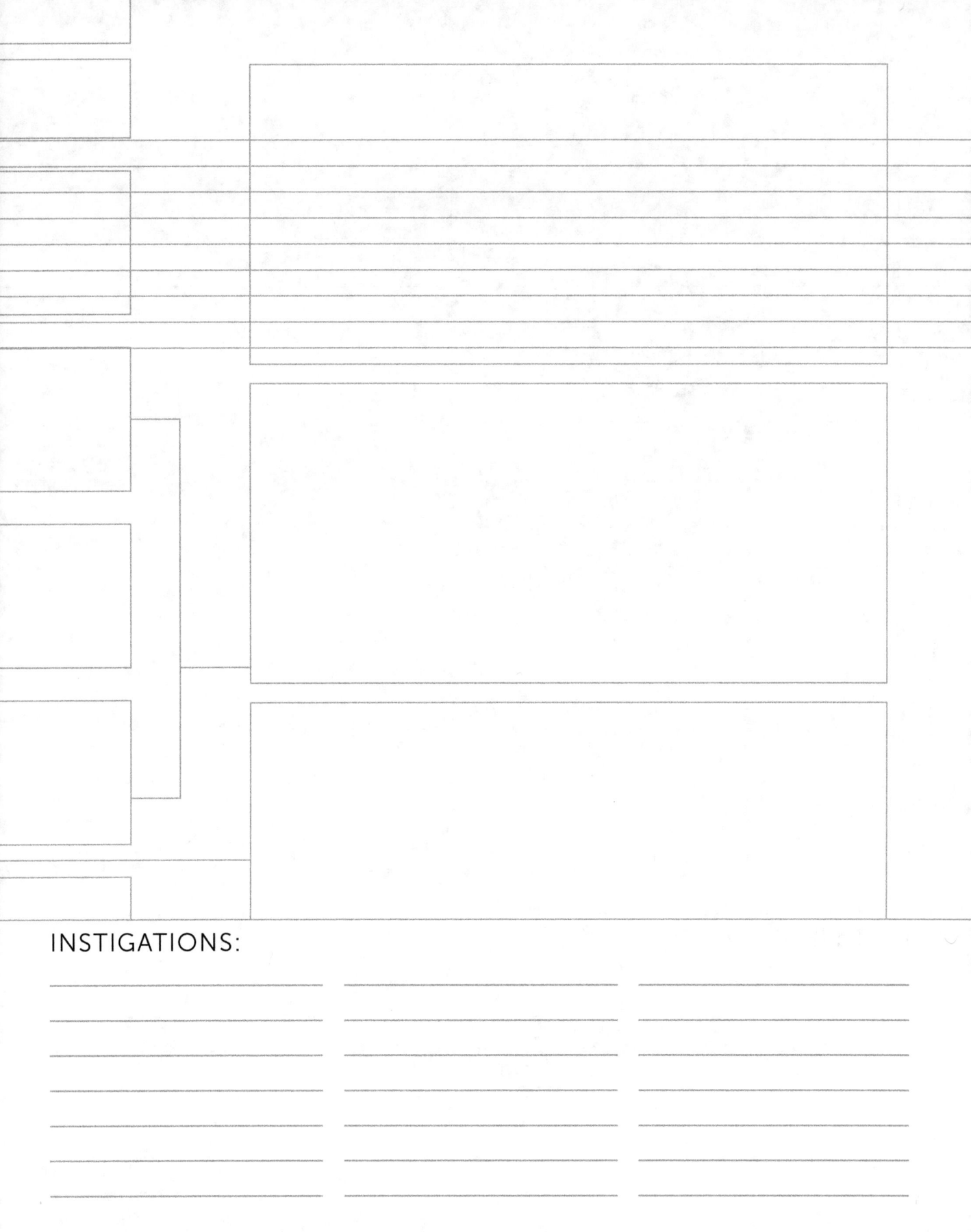

INSTIGATIONS:

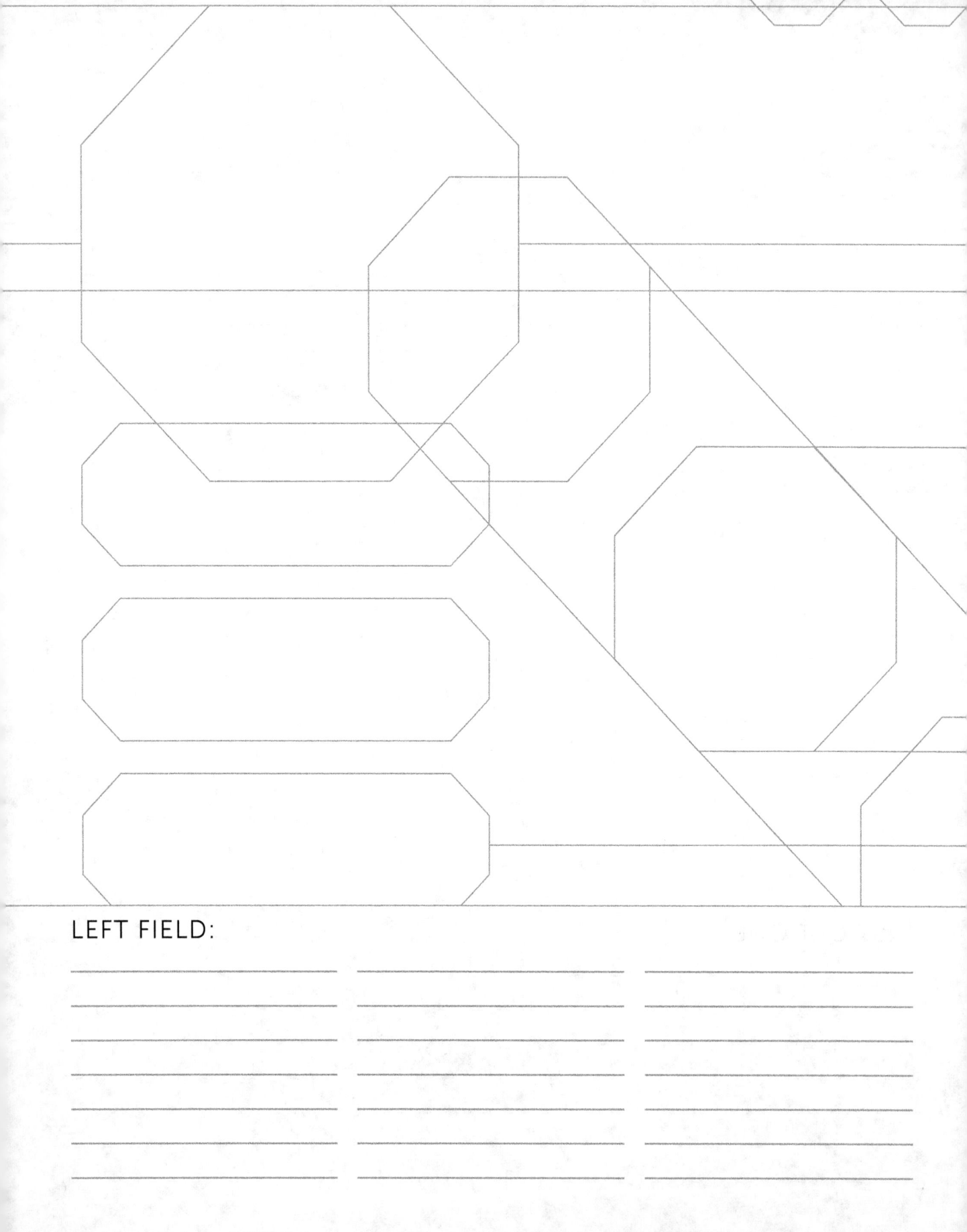

LEFT FIELD:

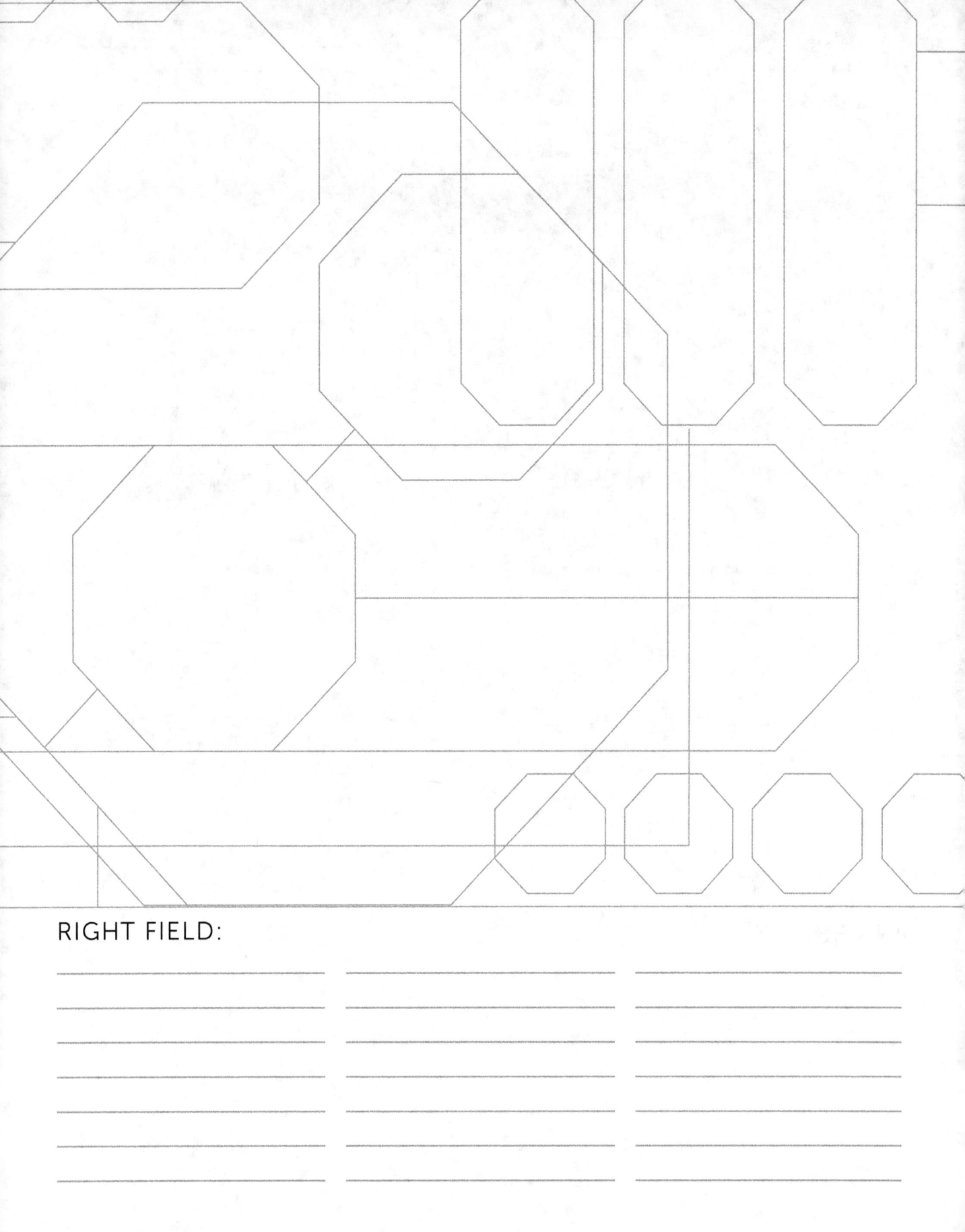

RIGHT FIELD:

IN THE BOX:

OUT OF THE BOX:

IDEAS:
_____ _____ _____
_____ _____ _____
_____ _____ _____
_____ _____ _____
_____ _____ _____
_____ _____ _____
_____ _____ _____

PROMPTS:

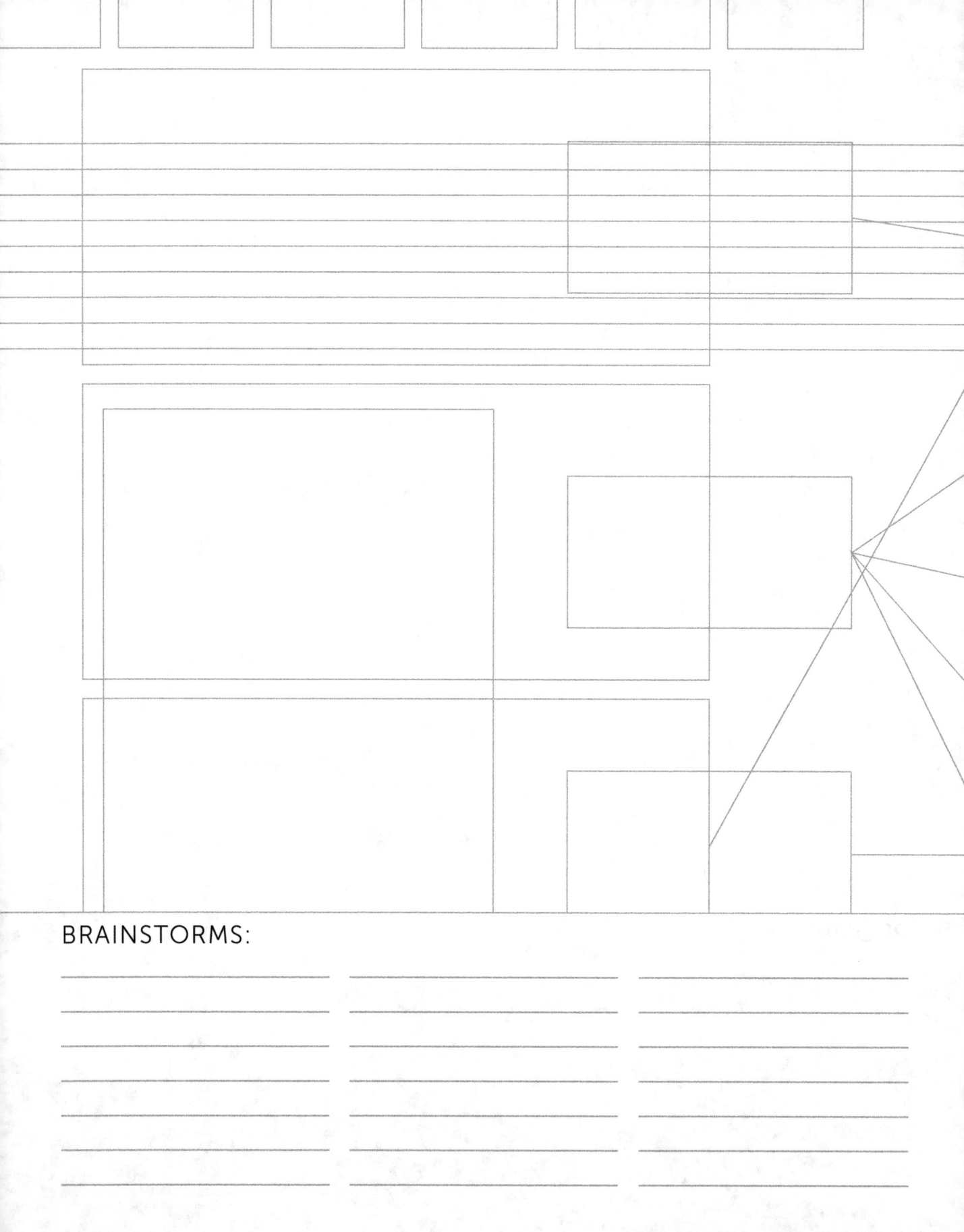

BRAINSTORMS:

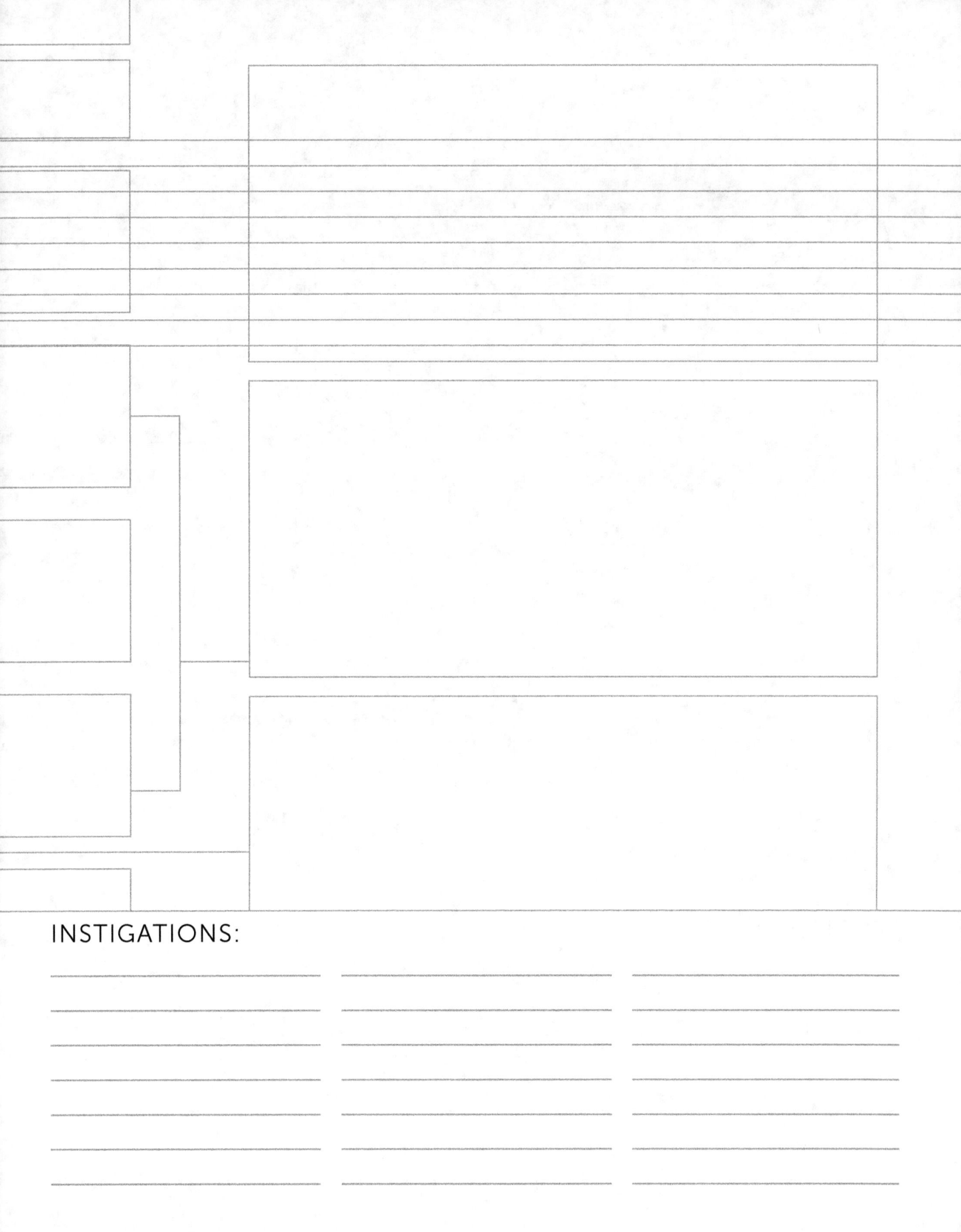

INSTIGATIONS:

LEFT FIELD:

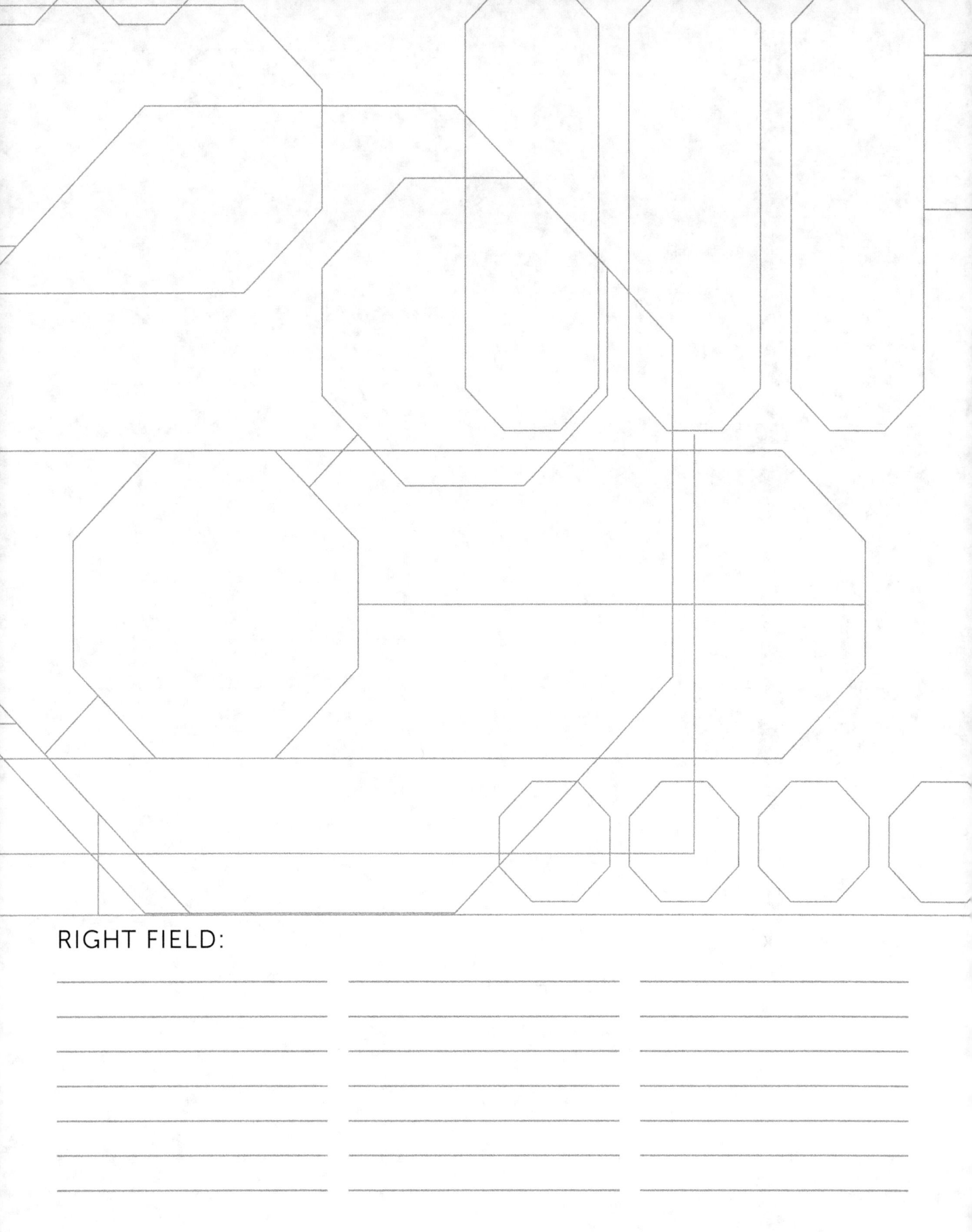

RIGHT FIELD:

IN THE BOX:

OUT OF THE BOX:

IDEAS:

PROMPTS:

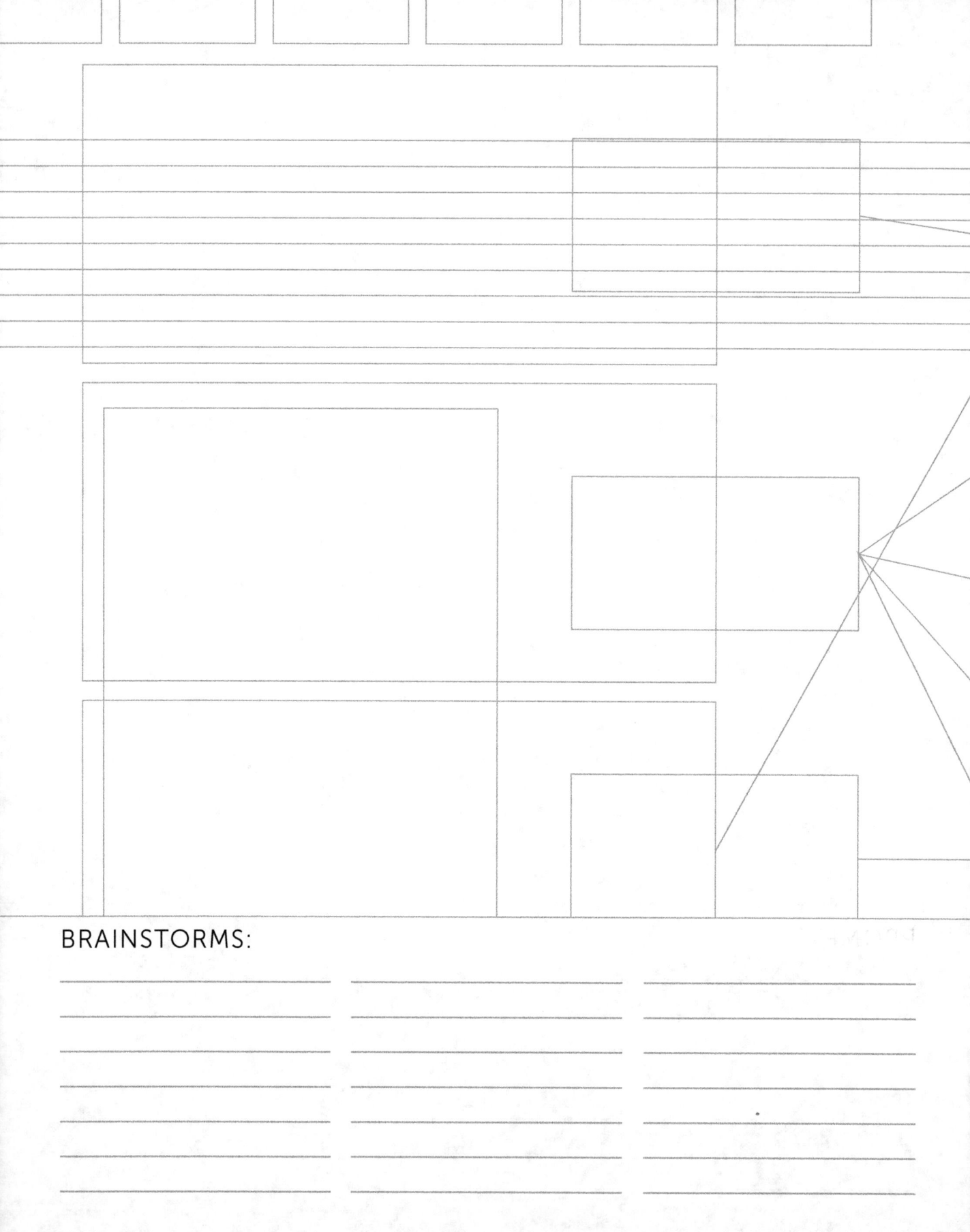

BRAINSTORMS:

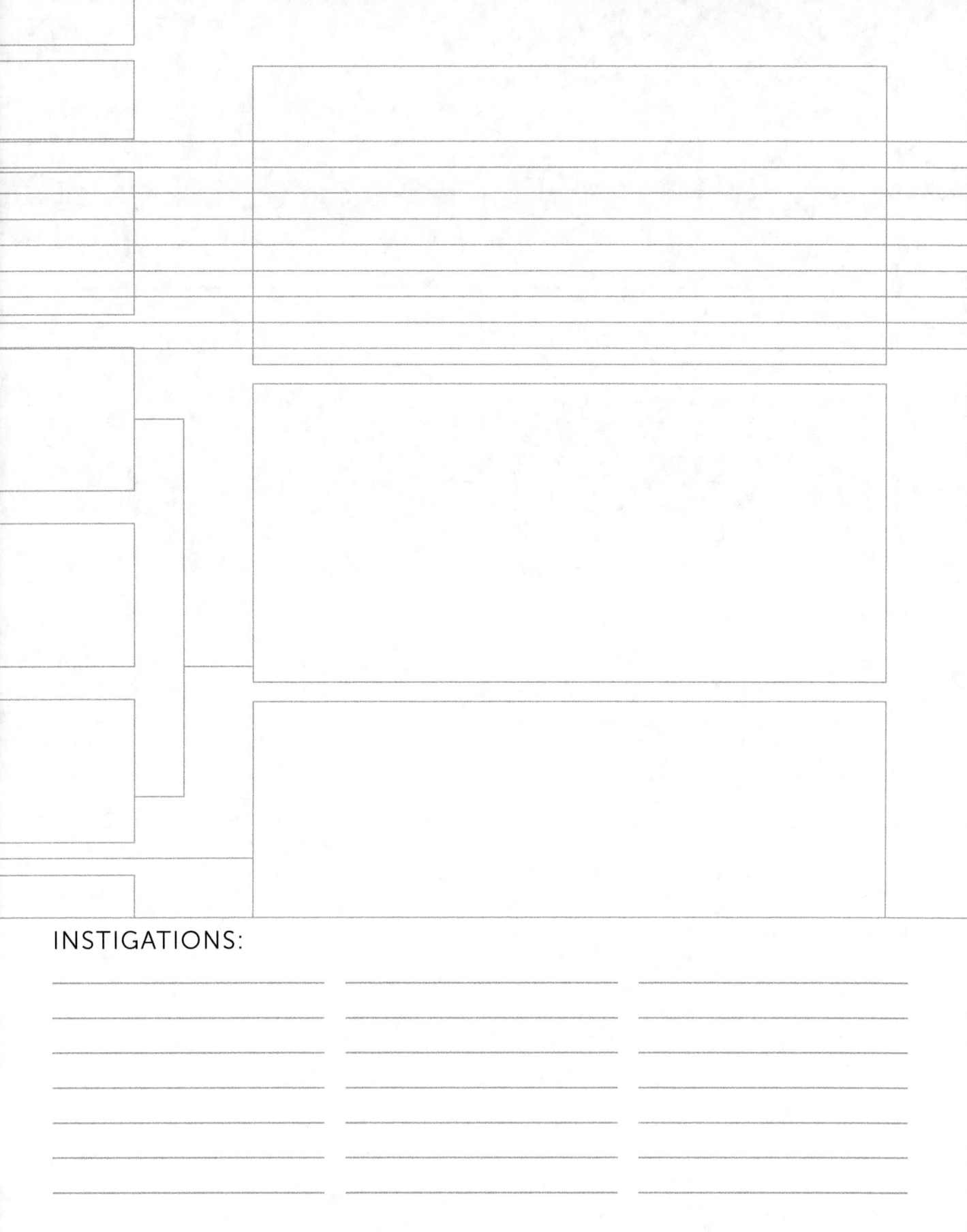

INSTIGATIONS:

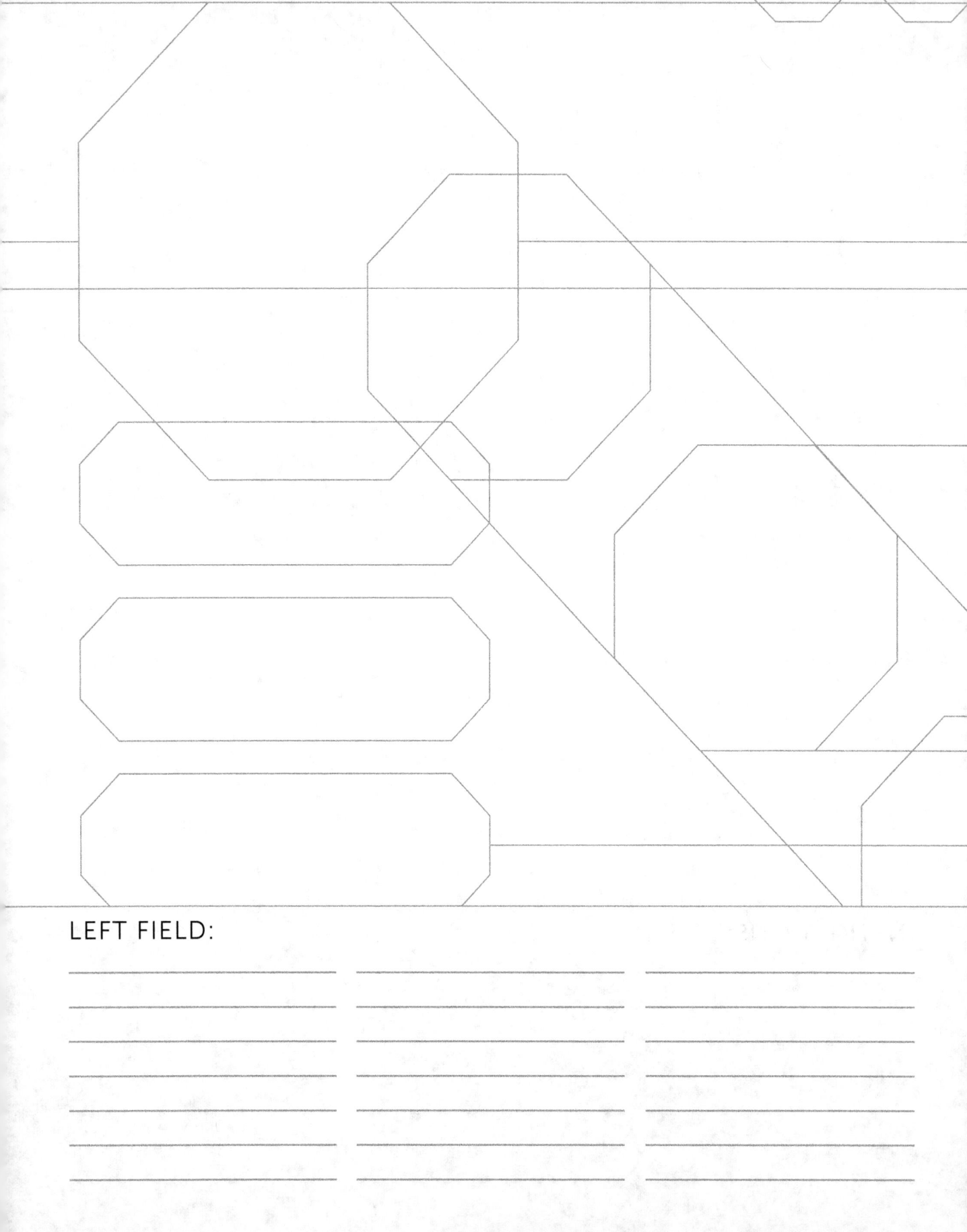

LEFT FIELD:

RIGHT FIELD:

IN THE BOX:

OUT OF THE BOX:

IDEAS:

PROMPTS:

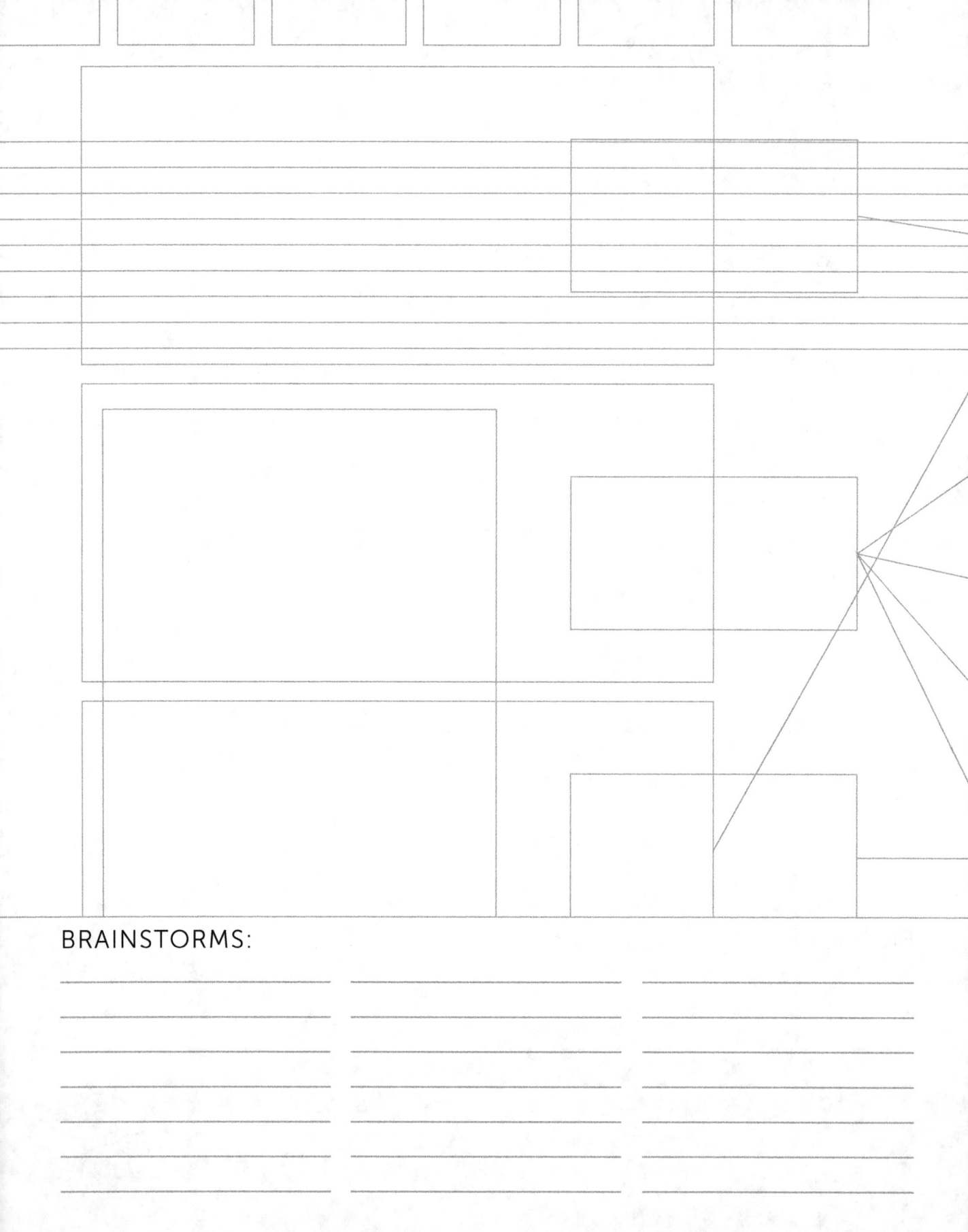

BRAINSTORMS:

INSTIGATIONS:

LEFT FIELD:

RIGHT FIELD:

IN THE BOX:

OUT OF THE BOX:

IN THE BOX:

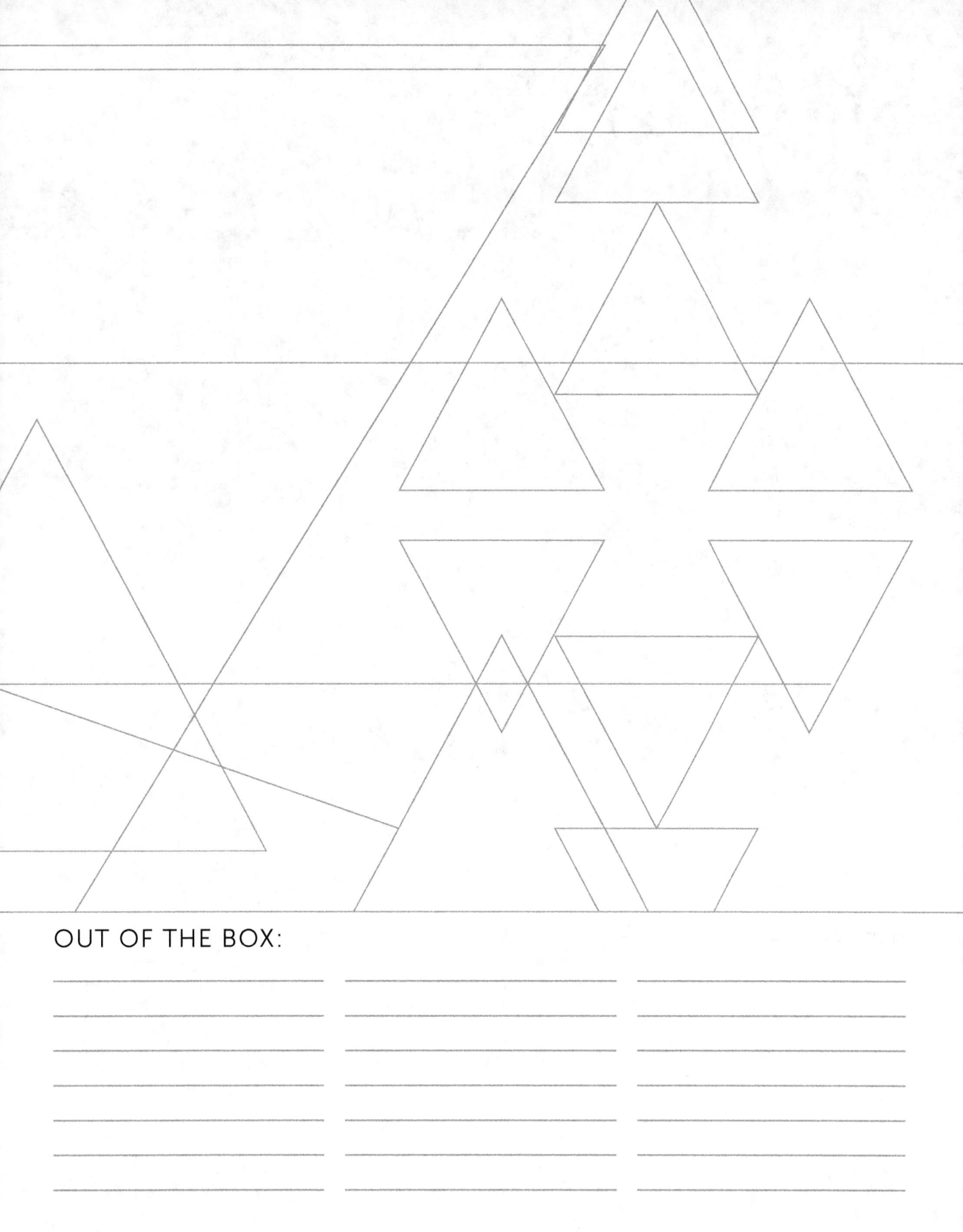

OUT OF THE BOX:

IDEAS:

PROMPTS:

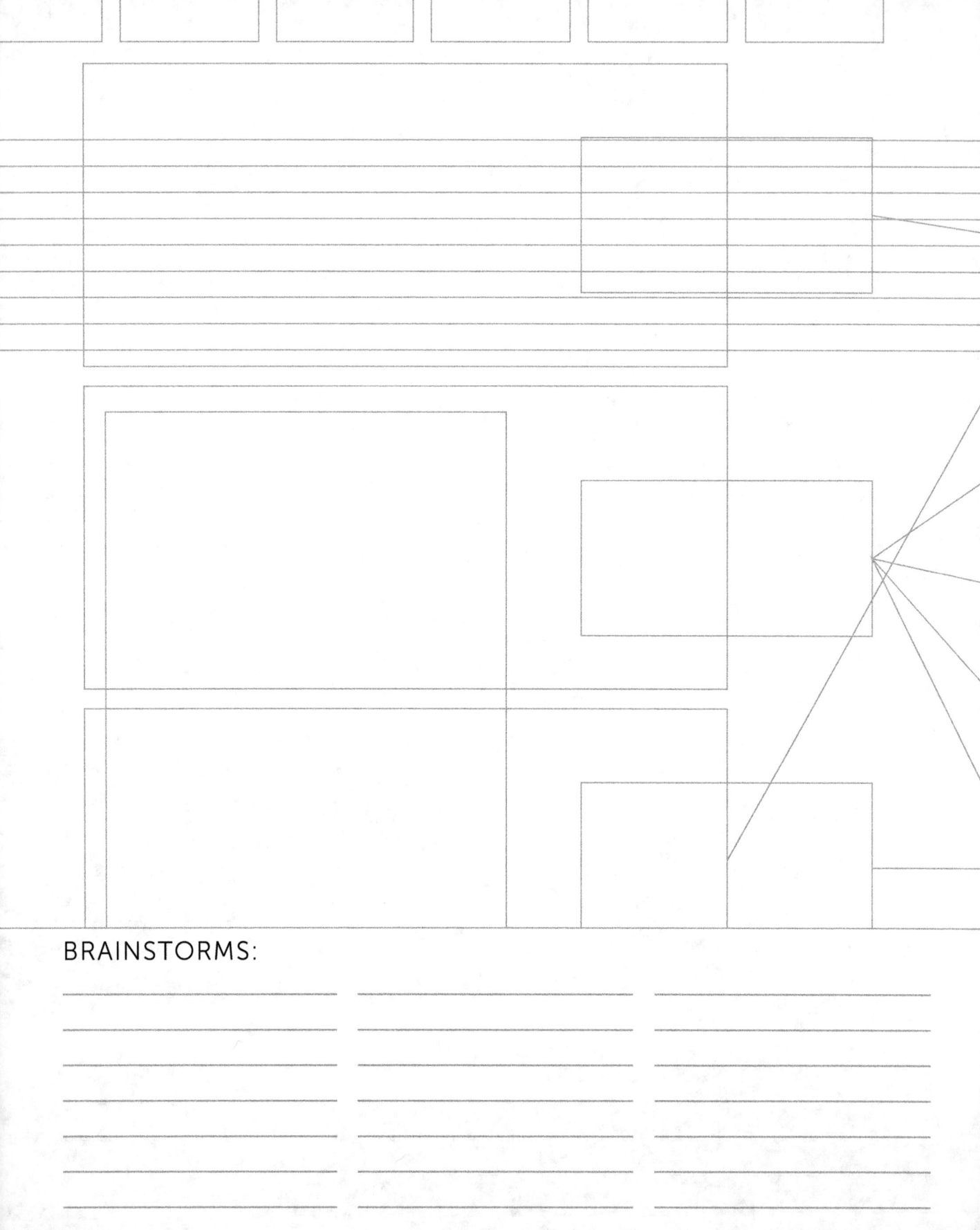

BRAINSTORMS:

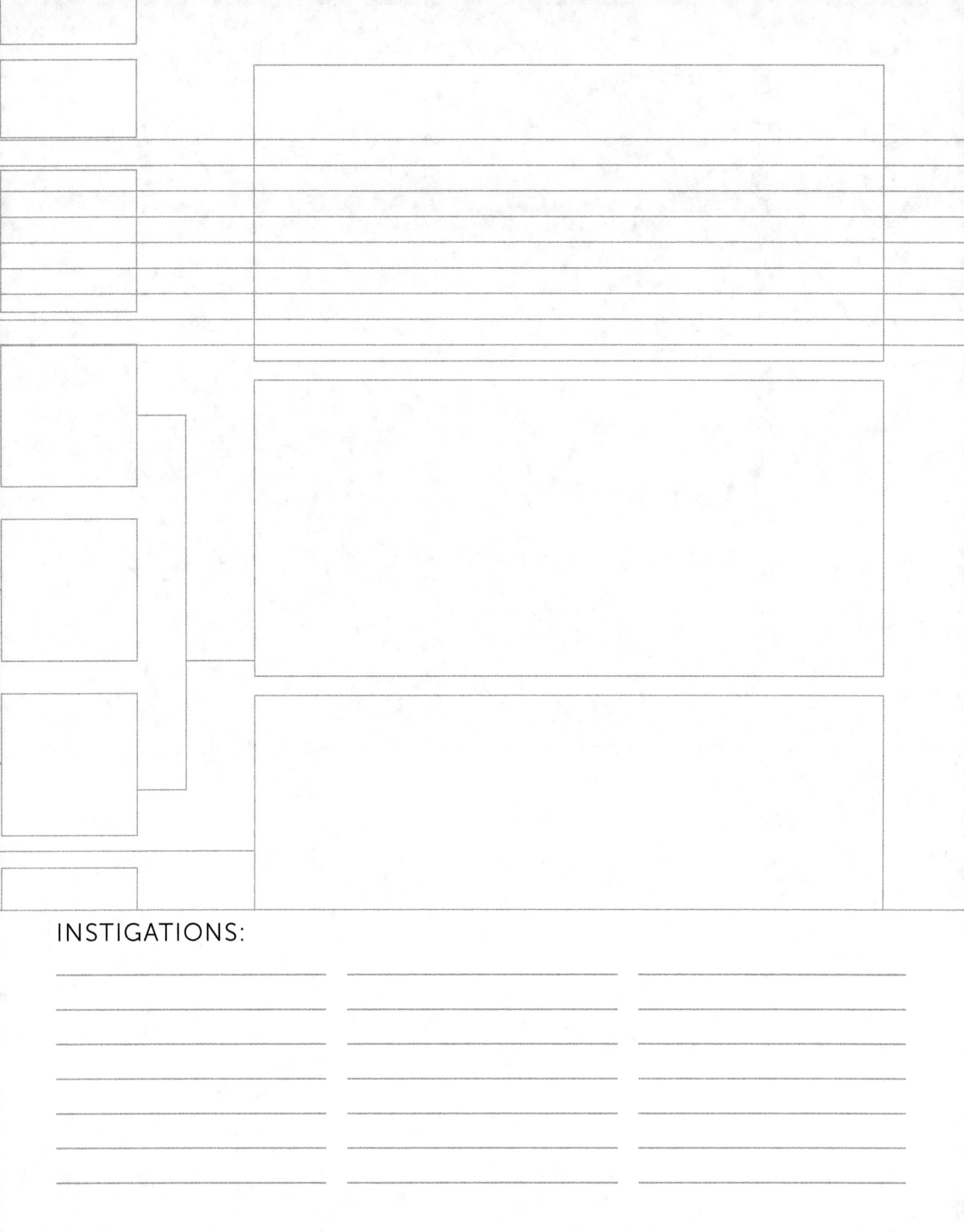

INSTIGATIONS:

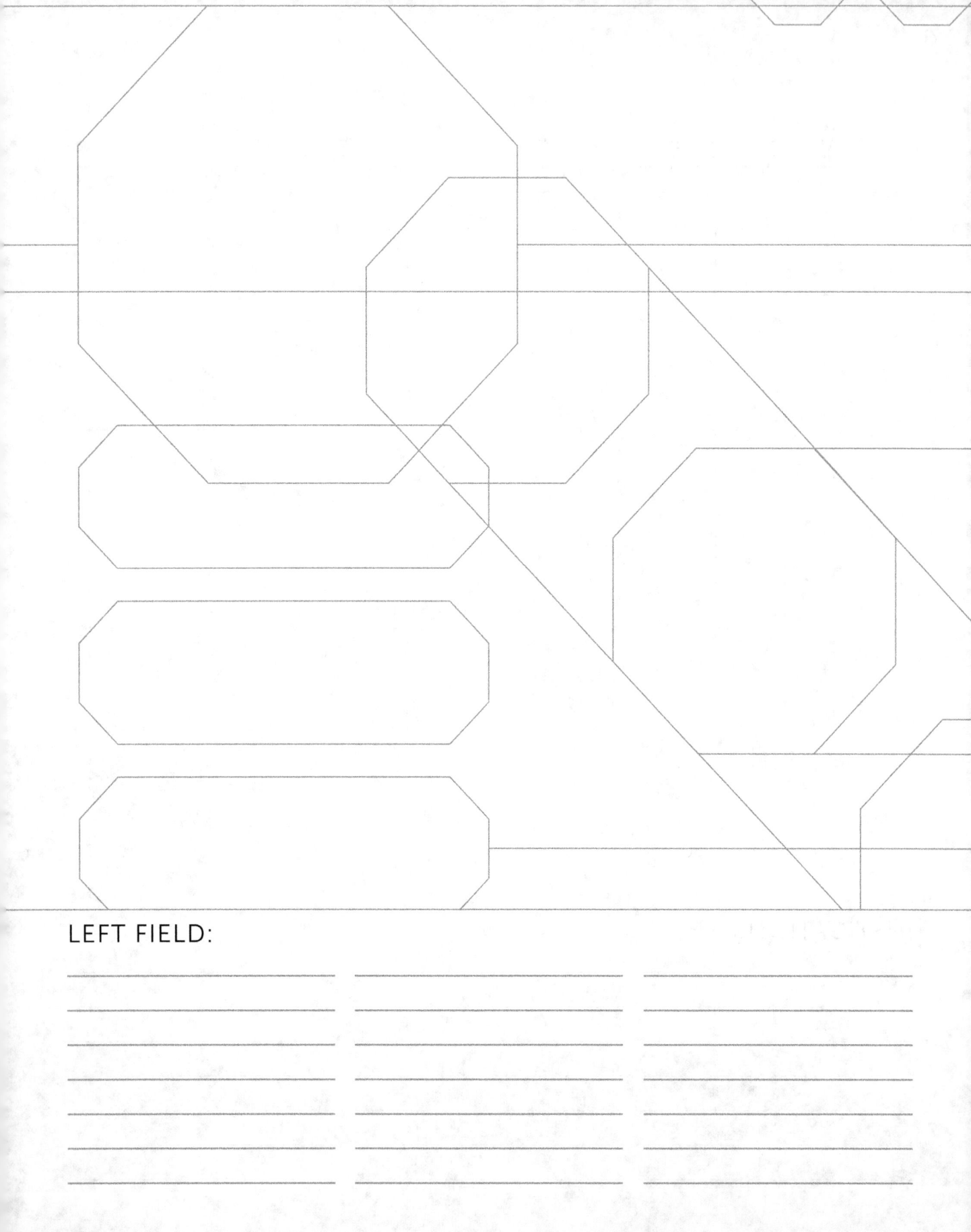

LEFT FIELD:

RIGHT FIELD:

IN THE BOX:

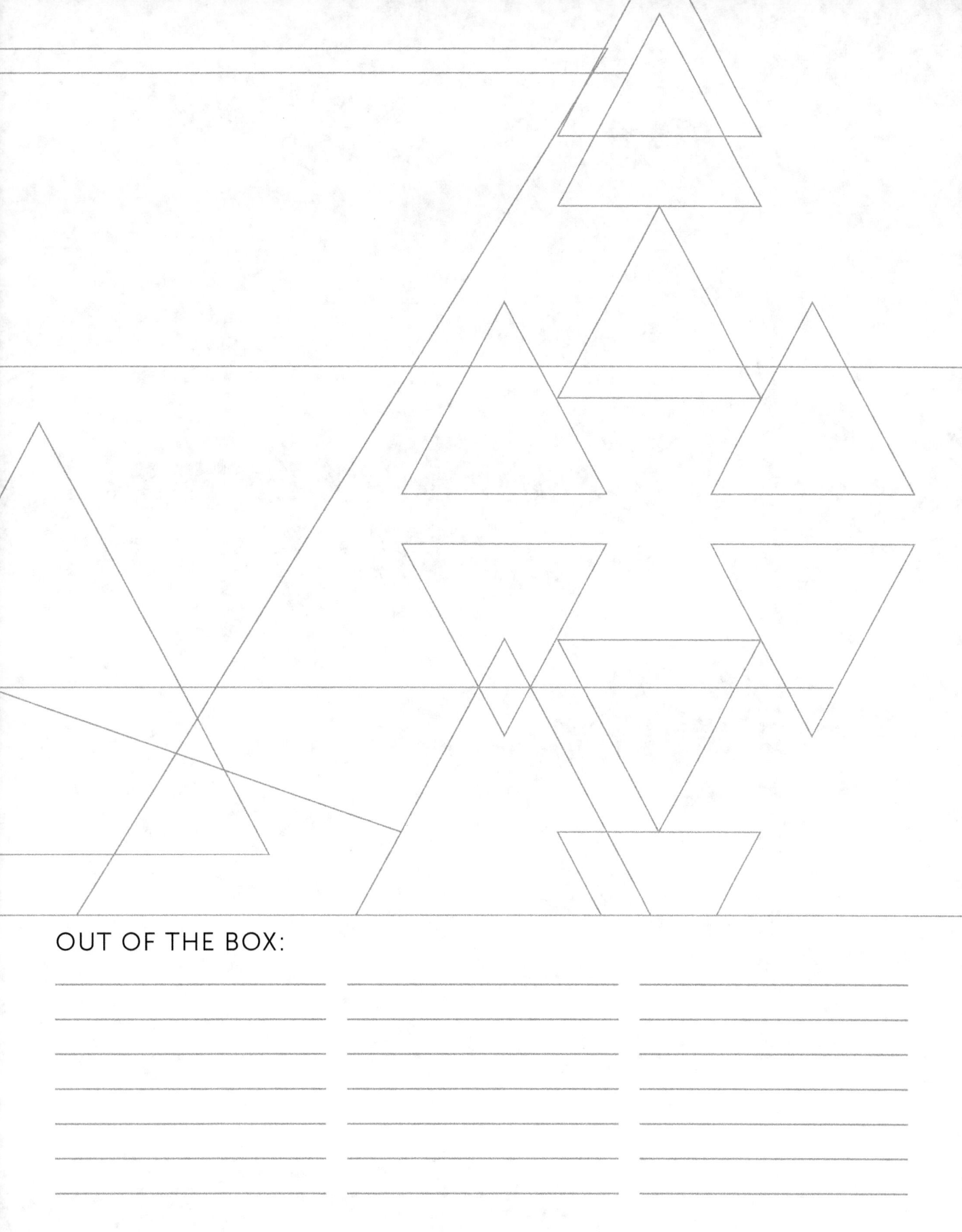

OUT OF THE BOX:

IDEAS:

PROMPTS:

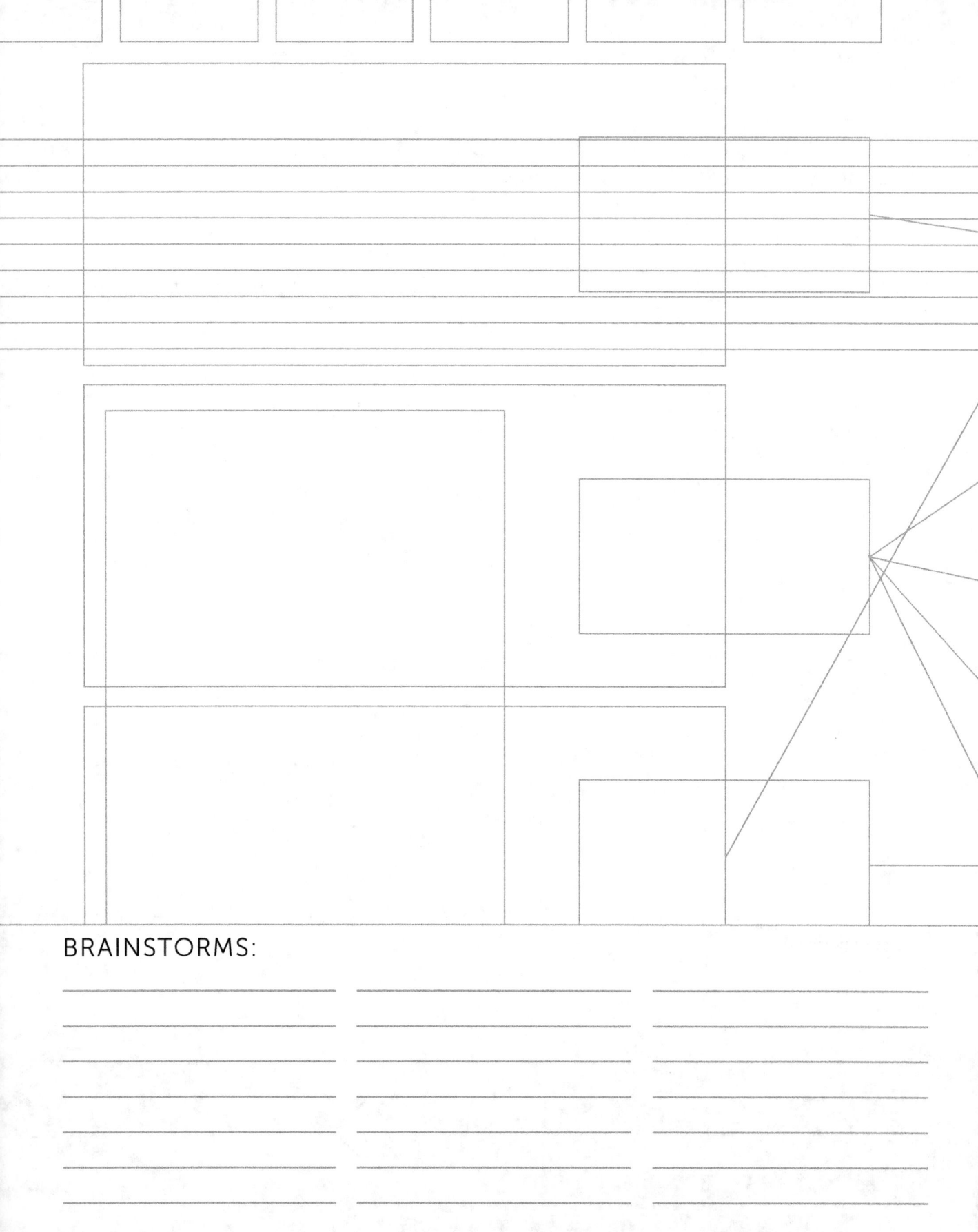

BRAINSTORMS:

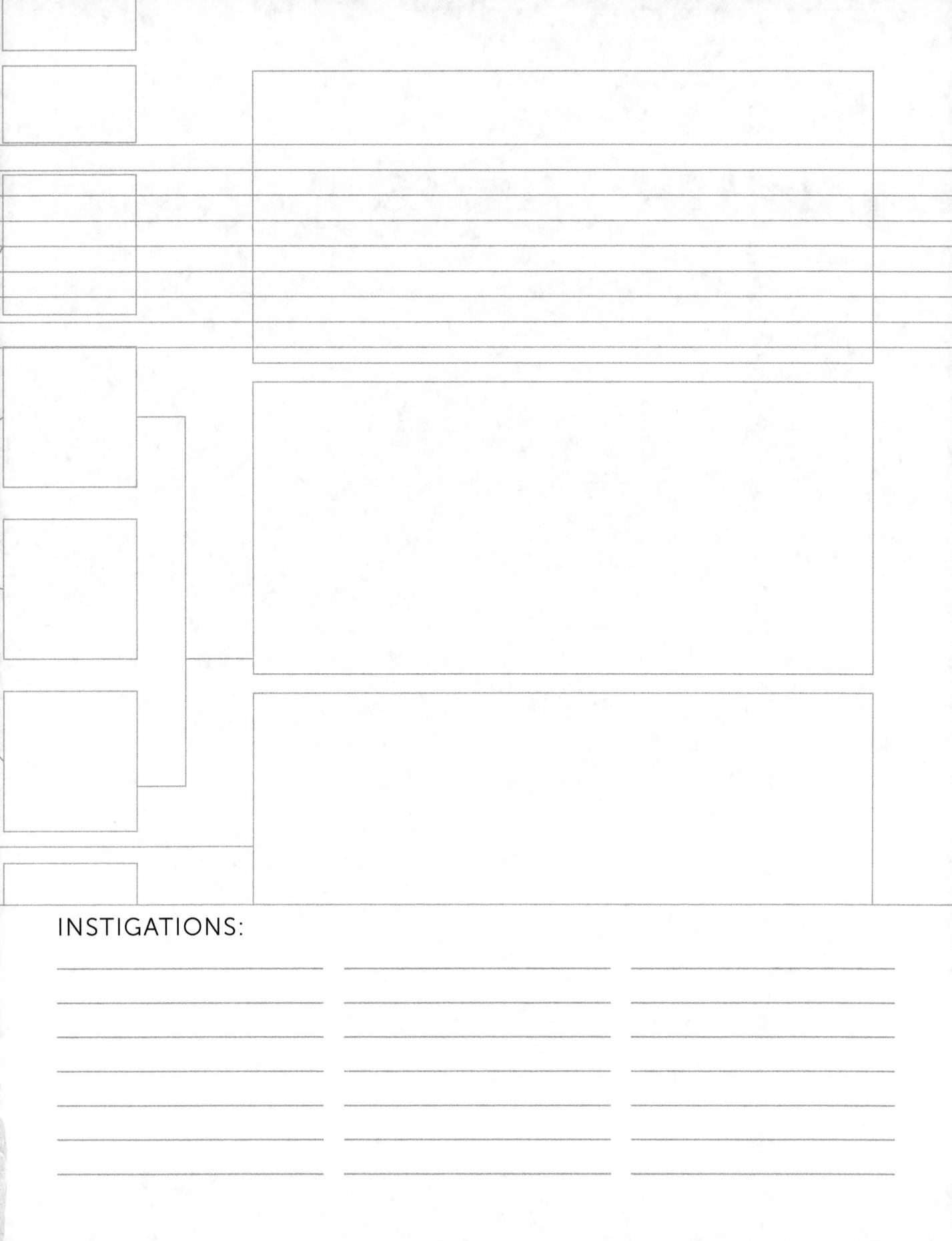

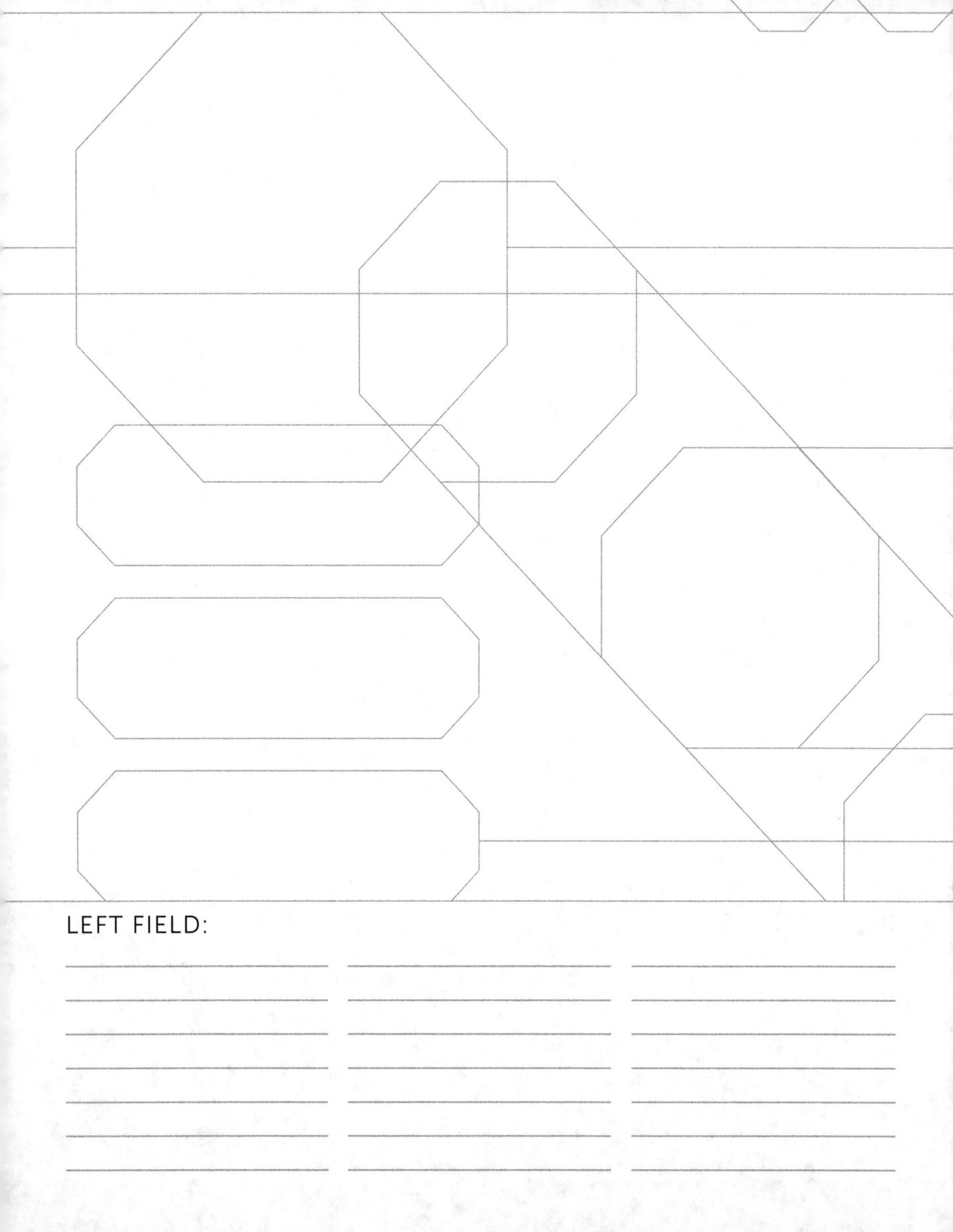

LEFT FIELD:

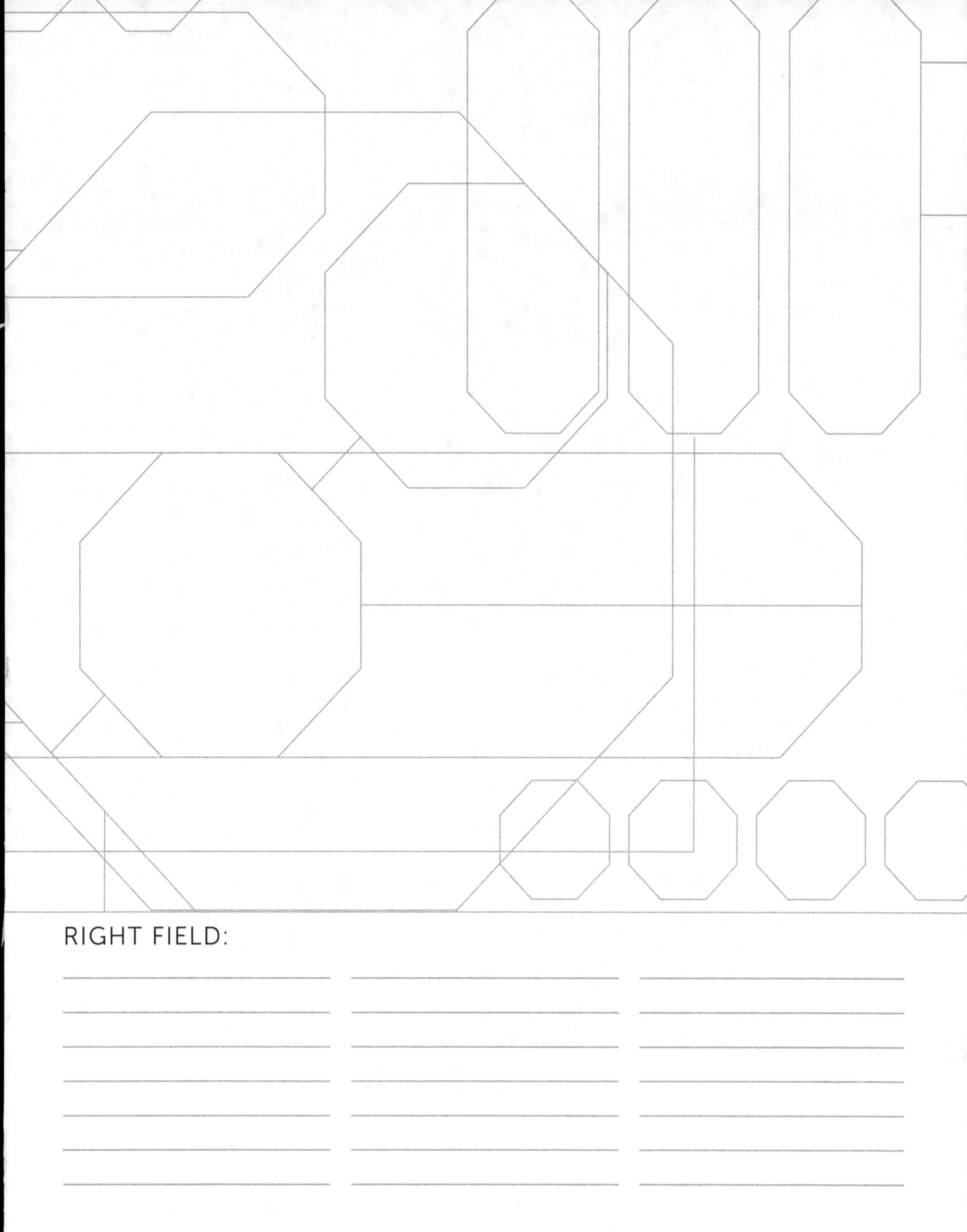

RIGHT FIELD:

IN THE BOX:

OUT OF THE BOX:

www.ingramcontent.com/pod-product-compliance
Lightning Source LLC
Chambersburg PA
CBHW060426220526
45465CB00008B/3028